Dedicated to: James M. Kerndt, O.C.S.O.

Monk of Our Lady of New Melleray Abbey
whose prayerful living is so simply and kindly shared

What do I know?

Color, sight, sound
Feel and taste

As my toes
Squish the warm, brown mud
Under sun-shined water

I splash
and laugh
as I taste and see
How sweet my Lord is

in my
puddles of knowing

I bring
my King

me.

And, sometimes He
comes and takes me

into His
Cloud of Unknowing

in the Son
we are one.

This I know.

Contents

Preface

Once long ago, a wise old philosopher said a wise thing (which philosophers are supposed to say). But he said it simply (which, often, they do not). What he said was this: "You cannot give what you do not have." Some people might say it this way: "You can't get blood out of a stone." That is why this book is—at once—so simple and so demanding: *You can't give what you don't have.*

You can't pray with children (of any age) unless you pray. Nor can you lead children in praying out of the stuff of everyday living unless you are reflectively aware of your everyday living. Nor can you ask the children faith questions unless you are willing to respond to the same questions, for they will ask you back. That they do so, is very good for all of us. Good, but not always easy.

Maybe you will discover it is more difficult for you to answer these questions than it is for them. Generally, children are far more simple and spontaneous than many of us. We adults have gone through so much living and so much education to help us survive and work in a complicated technological world, we live complex and complicated lives. It is difficult to be simple. Children are much closer to the creating of their simple, loving God. As yet their lives are not so complicated as ours. For them to turn back to their creating God's hand is not so long a journey as it is for us. They are closer to simplicity than we are—except those among us who might be very simply wise and holy. So it is a good thing to encourage children to spend quiet time with their God. Praying, however, is greatly helped when children are able to model and pray with someone. It is good for us to pray with our children.

Notice that I did not say, "Pray well," "Have frequent ecstasies," "Levitate at least once a month." All, I think, that is necessary is *to pray* and to be willing to be open with the children— to really pray, not to pretend to pray. Being phoney is such a waste of time. Besides, children smell phoniness. Besides again, it doesn't work with God. Being yourself, creature at ease with creator who loves us all, makes praying with children a delight—sometimes of awesome proportions.

For many of us adults, our religious or theological education has been highly cognitive. That is a good thing. But it is *inadequate* to the task of our relationship with God. We need an *affective* relationship with him. Probably we have more of a relationship with God than we are explicitly aware of. One way to become aware of our relationship with God, and to deepen it on an ever more mature level, is to pray with children. When we encourage children to come to know God in their heart, as well as their mind, and to be with God every living moment, then we ourselves will grow in our relationship with Him. Scripture tells us it is "in Him that we live and move and have our being." Let us enjoy that in our everyday living.

Assumptions about Children's Religious Development*

1. Children experience God. They may not articulate the experience well, they may not refer to it without encouragement, but they do experience God.

2. The child's experience of God is global in that it is both natural, and in that it is known by the child's total being.

3. Human development is not quite so full as it might be unless the religious dimension is attended to and growing. It is intrinsic to human health.

4. The language of the Judeo-Christian tradition is a fine agent for expressing the person's experience of God.

Be Aware

You can't give what you don't have,
but
you do have the experience of
having been a child!
Engaging children in our prayer heritage is
good for all of us!

*Paraphrased from *The Religious Potential of the Child,* Sofia Cavalletti, (Ramsey, New Jersey: Paulist Press, 1982).

Acknowledgments

Grateful acknowledgment is made to the following—

In St. Augustine's Cathedral Parish, Kalamazoo, Michigan:

- Father John Warner, Rector, whose concern for children's affective relationship with God prompted his inviting me to come and pray with the children, their teachers and their parents.
- Sister Mary Ann McCarron, S.S.J., Principal, whose cooperation in the venture contributed significantly to its success.
- the Teachers, who came with their students to pray, and who are a continuing source of encouragement.
- the Students, whose openness to contemplative prayer and relish of it, make being with them a reverent delight.

Ernie Nedder who, upon hearing Father Warner's vision, had one of his own: to make this work available to parents and teachers.

Sandy Hirstein, whose knowledge and enthusiasm bring a *joie de vivre* to the enterprise.

Jo Anne Marie Halpin, my lovely niece, who typed the manuscript with her customary laughing good humor.

Introduction

"Marlene, how do children learn to pray—and when?" The voice was concerned. And it was meant to provoke my interest. It did.

Father John went on. "Look at how children live today. Their whole lives are overscheduled: school, scouts, music lessons, Little League, band, swimming lessons, cheerleading, hockey, dance lessons, soccer. There is television which speaks, shows, images everything for them. All their days have an *exterior* orientation. God is interior. When do they have time to waste? Wasting time may have been a factor, a catalyst, for the longing for more in our lives when we were children. Wasting time allows us to know better our longing for God."

That was the beginning. "Don't answer me now. But will you think about coming here to pray with our children and the teachers—and eventually, the parents?"

The idea intrigued me. If prayer is relational, in terms of God and us, how did *we* come to know God? Children need to feed off others' relationships while forming their own. That takes time. Where do today's children have time? It takes modeling. Who, in addition to parents, might provide modeling for praying?

In addition, how can parents and teachers of children be encouraged and guided to make explicit what is implicit in their own relationships with God? How might they be invited to be consciously aware of this themselves, and to give this heritage, too, to their children? Especially when praying together is not in an adult's own childhood history, how might adults be helped to this extra and satisfying dimension of praying?

"What do you want to have happen with the children?" I asked John. "I would like them to have an attitude, an awareness of God's presence and providence in their lives," he answered. "And that," he added, "goes beyond intelligence into Mystery." I liked that. Years ago I taught in elementary and high school. For more years, however, I've been teaching in college, seminary, and adult education.

After some thought, I called or wrote to a dozen friends. They are people who know me, and who work with children.

"Do you think children can be taught to pray contemplatively?" I asked them. "And if so, do you think I could do it, beginning with five year olds?" Twelve out of twelve responded. They said things like this:

"Yes! Praying needs time and in a religious school you can manage to give it. It sounds important and right to me. I see a great need." (Mary, an elementary school principal in Brooklyn, New York)

"Yes! God bless the pastor who will pay for a teacher to do this! The teachers I meet are starved for prayer—once we start I can't peel them off. I think it's a great idea to have you praying with teachers and children." (Lil, a diocesan media person in New York)

"Yes! Lovely! Fortunate children! You have a remarkable combination of background to do it." (Leigh, author of children's books, Florida)

"Jump at the chance to do it! No one bothers to show kids how to do it. What a marvelous juxtaposition of children and adults!" (Joe, a college professor in New Jersey)

"Don't allow yourself to get swallowed by the parish," cautioned a father of four from Iowa. "Do attend to relationships with God and what the children actually experience."

"This is a most obvious need in the Church—this need for praying—and here is a concrete place to do it." (Keith, a Capuchin Priest in Detroit)

"It sounds right for the children and for you. Go!" (Ralph, Retreat Director in Indiana)

"Yes! This might well be the Church of the year 2,000." (Bob, a mid-western priest educator)

"You'd have such fun with the kids—and they, with you. It would do marvels for the kids I see." (Elaine, a social worker in Boston)

Twelve out of twelve said "yes," and "yes." All responded with enthusiasm, some with caution (time constraints, and—what about adults?). One, the Brooklyn principal, offered me the use of her school as a lab for a week in June. I went. I found reentry into the world of grade school remarkably easy, and was charmed all over again by the children, and by the generosity of teachers who were genuinely helpful to me and to the children.

In September we began a prayer room for grades Kindergarten to eight and some evening sessions for grades nine through twelve. This book is a record of the year.

For me the happiest results are these: Children asked teachers (and me, when they meet me in the hall), "When can we go back to the prayer room to pray again? I hope we can go soon!" Parents started to call or visit, saying, "My child says praying is the best subject in the school. What's happening?" Father John, the pastor, Sister Mary Ann, the principal, and I say: "Come and see— Feel the cloud of unknowing rain!"

Chapter 1

Where Will Your Body Fit?

(Praying at Home)

Where, in the place that you live, will your body fit? Where is a place that you like, where you can be private, where you can be alone with God? Where is a place where your body will fit?

These questions came from me at the end of the school year, to all of the children, from kindergarten through junior high. We had been enjoying praying together in a prayer room at about two week intervals since September. Many of the children were asking, "Will you be here next year? . . . Will we be able to come to the prayer room next year?"

I asked back, "What is it you like about the prayer room?" The answers came quickly: "The plants . . . quiet . . . the trees . . . the peace . . . the relaxation . . . the big pillows . . . the quiet . . . the slides and music (the little ones called slides, 'movies,' often enough) . . . the quiet . . . having God in my heart . . . just being here . . . peace and quiet . . . the stained glass unicorn . . . the quiet . . . being alone even though the other kids are here . . . the peace . . . being relaxed. . . ." From five years of age to fourteen, that was about the proportion of times "quiet" and "peace" were used. I had expected it of the older children, not of the little ones.

On the last day that each class would be in the prayer room before summer vacation, I checked with each, to see if I understood them right. "These are the things you like best: the peace and quiet, relaxing, having God in your heart." With verbal variations they all agreed.

"Well," I said, "if you like it so much, why don't you keep it up all summer? I don't know where you live. Perhaps you couldn't manage trees and a stained glass unicorn. Preparing slides and

1

music for you is my job as a teacher, but being quiet and enjoying God is something all of you can do by yourselves." So I asked: "Where in the place where you live will your body fit? A place you like where you can be private? A place where you can be alone with God in your heart?"

After a few moments I asked each child to tell another child what some possibilities might be. When a group looked puzzled, I primed the pump with examples which some of the children had already given me. Some of their stories follow.

Laura and Jean had come to my office a few weeks earlier, "Just to see you a minute." Laura went on to say that before she didn't think prayer was important, but she does now, so she prays more.

"When do you pray, Laura?" I asked her.

"On Wednesday nights."

"Why Wednesday nights?"

"Because that's when my mom and dad go square dancing and I have the living room all to myself. It's easier that way to be quiet with God."

"I pray on Saturday mornings," Jean chirped in.

"What makes Saturday mornings good for you?"

"I'm home all day. So I go up in the attic to be alone."

Jean grinned. Then she continued, "I go up after breakfast. The next thing I know my grandma is there saying, 'didn't I hear her calling me for lunch?' I didn't. She told my mom and we talked about it. I told her I was just thinking about God, and the next thing I knew, grandma was there. . . . You know, that makes me happy."

"I'm glad you are happy, Jean. What did your mom say?"

"Well, she said the attic was pretty bare, and she was going to throw out the living room chair as soon as the new lazy-boy came. Instead she put the old chair in the attic for me."

"How nice of her!"

Jean smiled.

"How do you spend the time?"

"Well . . . like last Saturday I was sitting there, looking out the window down on the apple tree. And I was thinking: 'God made the apple tree, but it has to grow from the inside. God made me and I have to grow from the inside, too.' Then I just sort of got quiet."

"Me, too." Laura intervened. "When I get quiet-like my mom and dad come home before I know it." She paused. "They are always surprised when the television is not on."

Then there is Billy.

"My dad and me fixed up a prayer room."

"Did you! Where?"

"In the basement. It was an old room my big brother used to use. He's married now. Do you know what?"

"No, what?"

The eight year old boy went on in a proud rush: "I make these things!" (he pointed to a banner). "I sew, and I make these things for my prayer room!"

I congratulated him and shared his pleasure. Billy left the room smiling.

So I told the class that some children like an empty living room; and another one uses her attic; one boy has a basement place. Where might they find a place to be quiet with God in their heart, a place where their body fits?

The little ones seem to like little places. "There is a closet in the kitchen . . . under my bed . . . under the cellar stairs . . . under my dad's desk, if he is not there . . . there's a kind of cubby hole in our bathroom ('Oops! Will people know you're there?' A grin) . . . in my bedroom closet . . . behind the living room drapes. . . ."

Children in the middle grades picked things like: "an upper bunk of an unused bunk bed" (my brother went to college so now I have the whole bunk bed to myself) . . . "behind my mom's clothes in the closet—they smell good!". . . "behind furniture" (like a piano, or where two couches meet in the family room, or the T.V.) . . . "between my brother's dresser and mine". . . "between the foot of my bed and"—(toy chest, closet, door, dresser—whatever was there.)

Older children also most often selected a part of their bedroom. One had a treehouse. Several mentioned trees, woods, the lake. But they knew that when summer came there would be a lot of people around unless they went early in the morning. One girl said her dog doesn't use his dog house very much and that maybe she could share it with him!

When it seemed the children had settled on a place, my next question was: "What will you bring, or put there, to make it a special place for you and God to be together? I think," I told them, "that it helps to get in the mood if you have something familiar around. At school we always have quiet prayer after slides and music. What can you manage at home?"

Most of the children picked a pillow. Some, a blanket or an area rug or a towel. The older ones talked about lighting a candle to help them focus. Appropriate cautions were issued—especially to the ones who talked about praying in a closet! A few said they would like to bring a picture they like. "A picture is fine," I said. "I like that idea; I do. Perhaps you might ask your mom or dad to hang it for you. No sense making a hole in the wall and starting out your prayer space unpleasantly. Ask someone to hang it at your eye level—your eye level for however you pray. If you sit, or kneel, or stand, or lie down—it will make a difference. Just make sure it is comfortable for you, so that the picture is a real help."

One little boy said he'd like to pray on the top of his bed. Him I especially urged to bring something, or use something, that makes it a special place. His head nodded affirmatively with solemnity. For the children who chose outside places, I suggested having a backup place for bad weather.

Other than that, it was very simple. And all of the children thought they could manage. I reminded them, as I do every session, that all we really need for prayer is our own *selves*. One little boy raised a question: "Don't we need other people? If we don't have other people, who can we pray for?" Praying does not need talent; we do not compete; there are no scores, or grades, or comparison with anyone else; nothing gets made or produced; we do not need money or equipment of any sort. It's nice and helpful to fix a place, but we do not really have to do that, either, you understand. They said they did.

Usually after we have discussed something such as, "where does your body fit?" I showed slides somehow symbolizing the topic, and the slides so used required music in the background.

This was the last time of the school year the children would be in the prayer room. I wanted to make it special for them. It also was the end of the school year, and the teachers were quite willing that I keep the children more than a half an hour.

4

"Why pray at all?" I asked the children again and again. Because it is an activity so inexpressive of our culture. Praying, like playing, are importantly useless. Finding a place where your body fits is incomplete without using it as a trysting place with God. But why pray at all?

It was here that we thought about our faith: we come from God, we return to God; living is journeying. During the journey it is a good thing to stay connected to our beginning and to our end. So we pray.

Children are marvelously open to receiving. They know their weakness, their powerlessness, their dependency for survival. As one sixth grade boy put it, speaking of his parents:

"I live in *their* house, I eat *their* food, I keep *their* rules—NOTH-ING is mine!"

Recognition of his dependency gets irksome to this child. That awareness of the experience of dependency is very present to him. He receives what he has. More, his very *being* is aware in a way many adults have let slip.

This boy is aware. Younger children are, too, and are simply open to acknowledge their received being. It is easy to turn them back to the God who made them.

The scripture which came to my mind for this last session is from the Book of Job, 12:10: *"He holds in His hands the soul of every living thing, and the breath of everyone's body."*

Now there is a good reason to stay consciously connected with God! He holds our lives in His hands, the breaths of our lives. And because God is a loving god, that is something to celebrate. Celebrate it we did on this last prayer day of the school year.

For this part of the prayer session I set up two carousels with a dissolve unit: one with slides of the children—five slides from each of the 17 classes. Children love seeing their own pictures. In their generosity they also love seeing each other: "That's my sister!" "That boy rides my school bus!" Little ones chant the names of the children whose images they recognize. God bless them!

On a second projector were other living things God holds in His hands: animals, trees, flowers, fruit, living water.

Of all of the music I used this year, the sound tract from *Chariots of Fire* was most loved. *Chariots of Fire* provided the musical background for our celebration of God's caring enough to hold our lives lovingly in His hands.

As usual, the shades were drawn. As usual, the children made themselves comfortable with big pillows, and turned their attention to the white wall which served as screen. As usual, those who had managed to secure a place in the recess of the doorless coatroom were smug with satisfaction. And as usual, they became quiet, enjoyed the slides and music—and, in this case, the celebration of the lives of living things, especially their own.

As the last slide (with the Job text on it) faded, and as I changed the tape to Zamfir's *Solitude,* the children prepared for prayer.

In our quiet prayer we do three things, simply. **First,** we ask God to come into our hearts. The first time I did this with the five year olds, Jerry scrunched up his face, pulled up his shirt, pulled up his undershirt, vigorously pounded his chest while mouthing: "Here it is, God! Here's my heart, God!—in here!" Usually I suggest they give God a tour of their hearts. "Use words, if you want; use feelings, if you want." "Can I use colors to color my heart?" "Sure!" Maybe you just want to *be* with God and you both know you both know. There are always some nods with that one. Do whatever suits you. Whatever you do, it is right. Between you and God in your heart, you *cannot* make a mistake. So communicate with him however you want, and give him a tour.

"Now be sure to show Him all of your heart—even those secret places you do not show anyone else, or would not know how to show anyone else even if you wanted to. Show Him anyway you want. Be together with Him."

Part of the "tour" includes a response to whatever we talked about earlier in the prayer room. "Let God know how you feel about that." Or, if the slides seem to evoke a greater response than usual, "Show God in your heart the slide you liked best . . . or didn't like . . . and look at it together. Let Him know what that slide might have meant to you . . . and listen."

After a few moments (maybe two or three full minutes—depending on the grade level, what else might be going on in the school, the changing weather, or an approaching holiday) we begin the **second** step. We tell the children: "Now put into your heart all the people who love you. You have a big heart, they will fit." Jimmy, another little boy, scrunched up his fists and grunted while

6

he pulled apart, in gesture, his heart. "Put into your heart all the people you love." (A little voice whispers, "Sister, my mom is having a baby soon. Can I put the baby in my heart even if it isn't here yet?") . . . "Now you and God look at them together. Is there anything special you want to tell God about anyone? Is there someone who is having a birthday, or someone who is sick, or getting married, or going away, or someone you've had a disagreement with? Whatever it might be God does know, but it is good for Him to know from you, so you tell Him now. And tell Him any way you want: in words, in feelings (or color), or just let Him know. . . . Now you and God look at the people you love and who love you, and *love them together*." (I think if parents saw the expressions on their childrens' faces at this part of the prayer, the wonder of their birth might flood them again to a new level of fulfillment.)

After a few more clock minutes we move to the **third** step: "Let the people fade, even though you and God keep on loving them. Remember God always is present, and always is loving us. What we need to do is to take the time to enjoy it. No matter who we are, no matter what we do or do not do, God always is loving us. Take these next few moments to *enjoy* God's loving you."

This is the longest prayer time. The older children sometimes take five, six or seven minutes before an eye opens and roams around the room to see what the others are doing. Even more beautiful (radiant might be a better word) than their faces a few moments before, are the faces now. Some are utterly serene, breathing as though asleep—although they are not. Some smile slightly. Some simply are radiant. And one might be absorbed in tying two others' shoe laces together, or looking at me with bright blue eyes while sticking a pin into the next child's sneaker.

In closing I remind them that they can do this anytime, anyplace. All they need is *themselves* and their willingness to be quiet and enjoy God's loving them. "For," I say to the children every time, "no one, absolutely no one, can give God your love but you. And no one, absolutely no one, can receive God's love for you except you. So it is important for you and God to enjoy each other's company."

Then I ask them to open their eyes gently, and to sit up if they aren't sitting. (Most of the children chose to lie on the carpeted floor and use the big pillows: some sit on them; a few kneel with head in knees. They choose their own posture: the only rule is that no one interfere with anyone.) We end by praying the Lord's Prayer together. At times we add a part of the text from the reflection, e.g., "The Lord is my Shepherd; I shall not want." I suggest they keep that text in their mind and heart as they leave. We went back to talking about summer places.

"When you have decided on a place at home, and what you will have there that is special for your being there with God, remember what we do together in the prayer room:

- We invite God into our hearts and give him a tour of whatever is going on in our lives;
- We put everyone who loves us, and whom we love, into our hearts and we and God love them together;
- We get quiet and enjoy God's loving us."

The children assured me they thought they could do that by themselves during the summer.

"One last thing," I told them. "If you do this everyday—or almost everyday—you are going to have questions. Please pay attention to them. It's good to talk things over with your friends, of course. Maybe the questions that come to you when you are alone with God will need discussing with older people, too—like your parents, or grandparents, or some relative; or Father John, or your teachers. One thing is very important: do ask, and do not give up until you have an answer."

"Even if I have to wait until September when we come back to the prayer room?" "Even if you have to wait. You might want to write it down so you don't forget it." A nod.

Sarah, who enjoys high status because she has three simultaneously missing front teeth, trudged into the prayer room pulling her mother behind. "I want you to meet my mom," she said, pushing back the thick blonde braid.

"You're the Prayer Sister?" the young woman asked. "This is the prayer room? Sarah talks so much about it!" Her eyes were scanning the room. Things seemed to check out.

"There is only one thing, Sister." There was a polite pause . . . a deep breath. "Sarah has found her private place to be with God in her heart." The little girl looked up at her mother and beamed. "But . . ." the woman continued, "do you think . . . well, does she have to have the bean bag chair under the dining room table? (in a rush) Do you think she could pray as well in her bean bag chair in her bedroom?"

"What do you think, Sarah?" I asked the little girl.

"I only use my bedroom to sleep in and to change my clothes, so I guess I could pray there."

Sarah's mother was pleased. I was relieved. And Sarah had found a place where her body fits.

In Summary

Suggestions

1. Find a place at home where you fit comfortably, and where you can be private.
2. Put, or bring, something there to make it special for prayer time.

Prayer Time

After becoming quiet in that special place, or place with a special thing for prayer:

1. Invite God into your heart.
   - Give Him a tour of what is happening in your life.
   - Show Him (in words, or feelings, or just by being together) even those secret places others don't know about.
2. Put into your heart everyone who loves you, and whom you love.
   - Let God know from you if there's anything special about anyone today.
   - You and God look at them, and love them together.
3. Remembering only you and God can give each other your love for each other,
   - be very quiet inside.
   - enjoy God's loving you.

4. At the end of the prayer time,
   * open your eyes and sit up slowly.
   * say the Lord's Prayer, slowly.
   * take a moment by yourself before doing other things again.

Be Aware

No one can give your love to God
   EXCEPT YOU.

No one can receive God's love for you
   EXCEPT YOU.

You and God are
   important to each other!

Chapter 2

Special Space

(An Environmental Note to Teachers)

If our relationship with God is a special relationship (and I am convinced that it is) then it is a good thing to have special space for special times of being with Him. As far as a school situation is concerned, I was given optimal circumstances. Suppose we look at what was done at St. Augustine's, and then consider other kinds of possibilities—since not all teachers have the same kind of room.

St. Augustine's new elementary school was leveled by a tornado three years before my arrival. The old school building was reactivated—not all of the rooms were in use. After roaming around the old building with the pastor and principal, and after considering a variety of possibilities, the kindergarten was moved and that room given over to being a prayer room. The prayer room is situated in a corner of the building tucked in between the principal's office and the secretary's. That means there is minimum traffic. It also means that we do not hear the hustle and bustle of classroom activities.

Carpeting was already on the floor. There was a small coat room with no doors. Immediately that recessed space made it a most desirable place for a child to be. Windows have shades—a real asset for using slides and other visuals.

"What I want," said the pastor, "is for the children to have an attitude, an awareness of God's presence and providence in their lives." Father John's theory about so many young people leaving the Church is that they have no *affective* relationship with God. "What can we do to promote that kind of relationship?"

"Environment is a start," I responded. "How simple and how pleasing can we make special space for the children?"

We stood there looking at the empty space, the white walls. "Living things," I said, "for lively children." Father John agreed. The choir master, who is also a superb gardener, went with me to a greenhouse. We purchased two weeping fig trees (the kind which often can be found in shopping malls). Four large standing plants (in the course of a year one part of one plant was broken off by a child leaning into it—the rest all remained intact) and two hanging plants. All the greenery is concentrated in one quarter of the room, immediately visible as the children walk in. Plants and trees form a kind of reading corner, with a low table, children's bibles, and a few appropriate books. As a reading corner, however, it was not used much except by children who spent recess time there, and parents waiting for their children after school.

The other large purchase was 30 large corduroy-covered pillows (on sale at a local discount store) in earth colors. They provide the occasion for one of the three rules operative in the prayer room: *one pillow each.* Boys, especially, seem to like the comfort and tend to build themselves couches. If they can, they take more pillows and wall themselves in. "One pillow." It's a constant effort to enforce that rule.

The room now contained green trees and plants; brown, tan, rust, and green pillows—and two blue ones. Some bright color was wanted. In one of the windows I placed a large square of stained glass: a white unicorn emerging from a very blue sea. There is a golden orb sun surrounded by a red sky. It is vividly stained glass and refracts over the plants, the floor, and the children, with moving beauty. In another window I placed an unusual crucifix. It is leaded together, rough chunks of amber and ruby glass. When the sun strikes that glass, the colors streak the room. It is a vivid and beautiful reminder for resurrection thoughts. Children like to sit in the puddles of color, second only to a place in the coat room.

That's all that's in the room, except for two low hassocks: one for the classroom teacher and one for me. I didn't want to sit as high above the children as a chair would place me; I did want to consider my lack of limberness with respect to floor pillows. So a hassock was the compromise. Besides, hassocks were on sale next to the pillows.

I want as much simple empty space as seems reasonable. My main reason is this: for prayer there is only one thing necessary—*ourselves.* The children bring only themselves to the prayer room. One principle and two important reasons influenced that decision.

The principle reason is that I am doing all within my knowledge and power to teach the children that they, and they alone in their very person, are good enough for the God who made them good. For God we do not need to perform, produce, compete. We are good enough *as is.* Growing better, I hope, but for today, good enough. What God wants is our loving and our receiving His love—with the implications of that unfolding as we live aware of His loving presence., For the little ones, love, trust, being happy fills them. With that as a foundation, an interiorized moral stance can grow firmly during the middle grade years. Commitment and relationships, a sense of offending and forgiving follows in older ones. Without the trusting and loving foundation, later stages take longer and may remain incomplete. One result of this, some teachers tell me, is that the children love the prayer room because It Is one place they know they can succeed. No matter what the time or place is, no matter what the social position or economic circumstances are, all we need for prayer is God and ourselves. It is a good start toward whatever *knowing* of God, God will call us to. That is the principle reason why I have been bringing nothing to the room and I provide nothing but plants, pillows, and beautifully colored glass.

There are also two other reasons. One is that I will not duplicate what the classroom and art teachers do with the children. In my estimation, that would be confusing or competitive on the one hand, and expensive in money and time on the other.

The second important reason is that personally I am singularly ungifted in art and music. Any intent to use them would result in failure. Consequently, I was saved the internal struggle of keeping the principle reason intact: for prayer we need only God and *ourselves* and that is quite satisfactory to God.

That is the *physical* environment.

Then there is the *emotional* environment. Emotional environment, I think, is crucial to motivation. Why would children—of any age—want to pray? What helps?

In the beginning, the children (and the teachers, too) were wary of coming to the prayer room. No one was quite sure what this was going to be like. (Truth to tell, neither was I. I had never done anything like this). I had, however, spent the last seven years of my life teaching in a seminary and coordinating continuing education for adults. On grant money from the Association of Theological Schools I spent considerable time and money learning how educated adults best learn—and using that knowledge to design and teach short term educational events for people in church ministry. While studying the principles of androgogy (adult learning) and contrasting them with principles of pedegogy (child learning), it seemed to me that children were being short changed.

True, children are not just miniature adults. Equally true, adults are not just uniformly adults from voting to retirement age. Human development is an ongoing process with discernable stages, succeeding each other from birth to death.

For human beings on any level, the best teaching takes into account the developmental stage of the person. That can turn things around. No longer is the primary question: "How can *I* best *teach* these persons?" but, "How do these *persons* best *learn*?" Then we, the teachers, adjust to their abilities in how we teach.

A long time ago the Greek philosopher, Aristotle, said much the same thing. In teaching we go to where the other person is, and lead him or her further. Since Aristotle was tutor to Alexander the Great, at least one of his pupils was eminently successful!

Methods, language, and timing clearly need adaptation not only to interest but to developmental and personal ability of the student. (Kindergarten children do not profit much from abstract ideas; the elderly find rapid brainstorming difficult.) My hypothesis, however, is that the circumstances so clearly delineated in adult education might well prove helpful in child education.

One of those principles, broadly stated, can be encapsulated in one term: *hospitality*—hospitality of place, hospitality of space, hospitality of heart—welcoming.

We have a welcoming God who "delights in His people." How do we welcome each other? If we have hospitable homes, what do we do there to welcome wanted guests? How can we transpose that welcoming to the children who come for prayer? Of course, a good deal of that depends on the personality of the host, hostess, or teacher. It needs to be an authentic expression of each one's own welcoming personality.

What I do in the prayer room is to start a cassette player with pleasing music before the class arrives at the door. (I use music which is pleasing to me: classical or semi-classical instrumental music.) I stand at the door welcoming the children to the prayer room, telling them I am pleased to see them, inviting them to take *one pillow, please,* (first rule); asking them to walk; and reminding them that only the first two can occupy the small coat room recess.

But I do welcome them. Teachers (who always are present with their respective classes) are a big help. Sharon, the kindergarten teacher, encourages the children to "walk on marshmallow feet." Other teachers give the boys and the girls, alternately, first entrance to select pillows. (No one color is a all-time popular color. I guess it's just getting there first and being able to choose a pillow from the bottom of the pile. It *is* an effort to keep urging, "This is the *prayer* room. There is no need to hurry. There is time for you to pick a pillow and get comfortable." Holidays, weather, and pending school activities have much to do with how successful a quiet settling it is—or isn't.

The *second* rule is: Each one has his or her own space. Even when we start out this way, it seems that whoever the children in the middle of the room are, they possess strong magnets which pull the others toward them. Every so often I need to encourage them to separate and have their own space, not touching each other.

Part of hospitality, as I see it, is for everyone to be comfortable. This brings up the *third* and last rule: No one interferes with anyone else. I invite the children to be comfortable. Some sit, some lie on stomach or backs, some curl up. The small ones, if they lie diagonally, fit their whole bodies on the pillow. If, in the beginning, I want to instruct on some point, I ask them to sit; later they can choose their own posture. This follows the advice of St. Ignatius of Loyola, who taught his people: Be comfortable enough that the body does not interfere with praying.

The first part of the session may take the form of brainstorming, or group work, or asking the children to tell experiences (children do have experiences and these experiences are gold mines for prayer). No matter what they offer, I accept. Adult education principles insist on the acceptance with acknowledgment but no criticism of what people offer for brainstorming. Besides, who can argue with a recounted experience? So no matter what the children say, I accept it. (Except when on a occasional testing, with some silly statement, I remind myself they are guests, and I am being hospitable, and I treat them as I would a guest: with a smile and moving on to the next person. Inattention can work wonders.)

Rarely, if ever, do I correct what children say. Always I affirm their experience. Sometimes I encourage a follow-up or an additional point of consideration from their experience. Never do I blame or try to extract a promise of any sort. That would be inappropriate for prayer.

Adult education principles consider facilitator and participant as co-learners. In the matter of prayer, of relationship to God, of facilitating children's coming to know God's love for them, are we not truly co-learners? Have they not the life of grace in them? I have come to trust the life in each human being, regardless of age, very much. Free from the fears of "being wrong," or "dumb," or "weird," or "stupid," or unacceptable in any way, their life rises to good for them which I can only witness and rejoice in. Did not Jesus say, "I have come to bring life, and life to the fullest?" (John 10:10) Encouraging *life* and watching it flourish is a great pleasure.

Hospitality of space and hospitality in welcoming *themselves,* makes the prayer room a special place. When asked, the children don't use these words. What they say they like about the prayer room is the peace and quiet, being able to rest. I like to think that what contributes to the peace and rest is not needing to be self-protective or defensive. And when the session is over, again I put music on the cassette player and stand at the door thanking the children for coming, telling them how much I enjoy their company, and hoping out loud they will come back soon. Usually they say they will.

Pat, the sixth grade teacher, told me she tries to schedule the prayer room as the last period on an available day. "Why?" I asked her. "Because the children always leave happy. They don't fight, tease, or get upset in the prayer room. I like to send them home happy to their parents."

It is my fortunate situation to be involved in the school only in the capacity of prayer room—a very special space. Most schools I know of do not have such a room, nor do they have one person designated to pray with children and teachers. What can classroom teachers do, if they want to make special space for prayer time? (I mean this as times other than those when exclusively memorized and recited prayers are used.)

What can classroom teachers do, in way of special space, and in way of special hospitality for this time? *The Religious Potential of the Child** by Sofia Cavalletti has many specific suggestions for classroom teachers.

Some teachers said, "What about going outside? . . . What about the church? behind the altar? the sacristy?"

Whatever the physical restraints and arrangements, the space should be special, used only at prayer time. Most special of all, I think, is the teacher's attitude and the teacher's being the model of a person—the *hospitality* of the teacher's heart.

Sometimes being a model is uncomfortable for teachers. Cognatively, it is fine. In practice, there might be some uncertainty and embarrassment.

We talked about that—teachers and I have. More of an influence than any single factor I have discovered is the teacher's own prayer history. Many say that in their childhood homes, prayer may have been present, or encouraged, or "there was a drive for prayer," but it was not a spontaneous sharing. (Except for a "God bless you" after a sneeze.) Teachers express a dislike for superficial, or for "pushbutton prayer" because "you're on stage now and expected to lead in prayer." I find that kind of integrity beautiful.

Culture and childhood family have a great deal to do with our self-expectations. So seeing oneself as helping others pray (this may include using memorized prayers, but does not stop there; it is not a case of prayers, but of prayer) is beyond the self-expectation of many. Often enough it requires a re-examining of

---

*Sofia Cavalletti, *The Religious Potential of the Child* (Ramsey, New Jersey: Paulist Press, 1982).

one's relationship with God and a willingness to facilitate that relationship for others.

It is not complicated; neither is it easy—this hospitality of space of the heart. The chapter on prayer will continue to address the matter.

In Summary

Hospitality of Place

1. pleasing (plants, color, comfort)
2. simple, uncluttered

Even with hospitality, there are rules for the children:

1. sharing: one pillow each
2. comfort: own space; posture as pleases
3. caring: no interference with any other person

Hospitality of Atmosphere

Motivation depends on emotion, emotion depends on attitude. Motivation for prayer, in the prayer room, begins with an attitude of:

Welcome!

1. **Welcome** verbally; express pleasure at the children's presence.
2. **Welcome** with music.
3. **Welcome** the children's accounts of their experiences; their questions.
4. *With* them, **welcome** God among us.

God made us good.

Each one of us is good enough for the
God who made us good.

To please Him, we need not perform, produce, compete, or
"be good at" something.

Being good
   is
good enough!

Chapter 3
Milkstools

(Kinds of Praying)

"How many know what a milkstool is?" was my opening question the first time the children came to the prayer room. Some children in every class did. Either they came from farms, or they had visited grandparents or other relatives on farms. Not everyone knew.

"Why don't those who do know what a milkstool is tell the other children who never visited a barn with dairy cattle?"

"It's small . . . you know, low."

"There's a seat."

"It's got three legs."

"It doesn't have a back."

"You sit on it to milk the cows, if you don't have a machine to do it."

"What's important about the three legs?" I asked.

There was a long pause. Usually someone volunteered, "They have to be the same size."

"And if they aren't?"

Grins. "You'd fall off."

"Right! Or it would take a lot of effort to keep your balance, and you'd probably get a cramp in your leg." They agreed. "Can everyone picture a milkstool?" I asked. The children said yes, but they were looking at me with some doubt and wariness.

"I think prayer is like a milkstool. It has three parts, like three legs. If they aren't all attended to, like they have to be the same length for the stool to be useful, then it is hard to keep your balance.

"The first leg is private prayer, praying to God in your heart, alone with Him. That kind of prayer we can pray anywhere, anytime. All we need for private prayer is God and ourselves. That's the kind of prayer we are mostly going to talk about in this room.

"The second leg of the prayer milkstool is praying with a group of people, some people we know. That's like when we pray with our family, or class, or some other group." The children were nodding, waiting.

"The third leg of the milkstool is praying in church in a formal liturgy. There is something in the human spirit which wants ceremony and ritual, a kind of praying with many people—even if we don't know them personally—all worshipping the same God together. Besides, there is something comforting about knowing what's going to come next, knowing the prayers, and hearing God's Word with other people who also believe.

"Like the milkstool which has three legs of equal length—because if it doesn't we fall off—we need three ways of praying: alone with God, with a few other people whom we know, in church with many other people. We need to balance those three ways in our lives.

"Here, in the prayer room, what we are going to do is pray to God in our hearts. Before we start that, let me ask you a question.

"Think for a moment. When do you pray? . . . Are some of you willing to say out loud just one of the times that you pray?"

"I pray in the night before I go to bed.". . . "In my house we say grace before meals.". . . "We have a blessing in my house, too.". . . "I pray when my grandma is sick.". . . "I pray when I've been bad.". . . "I prayed for my kitten when she died.". . . "I pray when we have tests in school.". . . "When I broke my wrist skating.". . . "When the weather looks like a tornado, I pray for protection.". . . "When I break something in the house.". . . "For my uncle who died last week.". . . "When I sin.". . . "For my dad's job.". . . "For anybody who's sick—or in trouble.". . . "So we don't have nuclear war.". . . "When I had a sore." (A scraped knee was brought up for me to look at.)

Throughout the seventeen classes in this elementary school the litany was quite consistent: morning and evening prayers, blessing before (seldom after) meals; most prayers were said for those ill, dying or dead, in trouble, or when afraid. Some of the children seemed very conscious of sinning. "Not bad," I thought. "But not good enough, either."

There seemed little notion of the everydayness of being with God. I checked that out with some of the classroom teachers. They all voiced the same concern: It seems that children quite easily turn to God when sad or afraid or in trouble, but not many other times.

"How do you pray?" was my next question. After a moment's reflection they started to volunteer answers: "standing". . . "sitting". . . "kneeling". . . "when I'm bad I say I'm sorry" (and when you are good what do you say? Judy looked absolutely bewildered).

"That's fine. Every answer given is right. We pray whenever we want to, and when we pray alone we pray anyway we want to. Whatever we do with God in our heart is right, as long as we are not trying to pretend with God. Pretending with God would not work anyway, would it?" They all agreed it surely would not.

"I have one more question before we do something different." The children shifted on their big pillows.

"How do you know when someone loves you? Think about that for a moment. How do you know when someone loves you?"

"That's easy! They're nice to you!". . . "They buy you things.". . . "They play computer games with you.". . . "They do things for you, like make snacks.". . . "They take you places.". . . "They play with you.". . . "My mom makes my lunch everyday.". . . "They tell you they love you.". . . "Grandma gives me a hug.". . . "My dad plays catch with me.". . . "You fool around together.". . . "They wash your clothes.". . . "When you got a real friend you do a lot of nothing together." Of all the suggestions that last one, *"doing a lot of nothing together"* got the most smiles, nods, and "yesses" from the other children.

"Are you sure that that is how you can tell that people love you?" They were sure. "Then," I asked, "what's so different with God? Think about the things that you and your classmates said: how could you do those things with God?"

The idea seemed new to some of them. "Well, He gives us everything—like our moms and dads." "And food!"

"Yes, and that's a great and good thing. Tell me, what is your favorite way of knowing that someone loves you?"

Answers varied, but the cluster of answers which was strongest was *being with the person, just knowing that "they like having you around."*

"Oh," I smiled. "You are so very right! And that's one of the best things about God. He's always around. Not only that, but He is always loving us, and likes to have us around. Do you know what the Bible says about that? It says, 'God *delights* to be with His people.' So we are really sure about that. I'd like it very much if between now and the next time you come to the prayer room you thought some more about this. If God is always around, always loving us, always has time to listen, what other ways might you want to pray?"

Silence. "For now, that's enough. Let's do something different for the last part of your visit today." The children, for the most part, looked mildly interested.

It was the first time they had come to the newly established prayer room. It was the first time they had come to the room which had no furniture except thirty large pillows. They had looked surprised when they were greeted by me at the door, with nothing in sight but a pair of weeping fig trees and some large plants, and that big pile of pillows. Music was playing. (For this opening session I used the first volume of *Praise Strings*—no vocal, just instrumental music).

As they came in—a bit wary, a bit curious, and obviously having been warned to be on their best behavior—I invited them to select a pillow and find their own space to be with it. They did so. When they clustered, entangled feet, or started to lock hands for arm wrestling, I definitely encouraged them to find their *own* space, because it would be an important thing for them. "Besides," I usually add, "It is very important to be fair with each other, and it is unfair to interfere with another person in this room." That began to take root in them. Children are very sensitive to what is "fair" and "unfair."

Both students and teachers were a bit cautious. Some teachers told me later they thought I was coming to teach them how to teach, and what was the matter with the way they were teaching? As far as I know, nothing. And no, that is not why I am here. There is no criticism directed against teachers. What there was was the pastor's conviction that, if children could build an affective relationship with God, if that relationship were built well—positively, and with affirmation, children would be more likely to live their baptismal consecration more consciously all their lives.

"What I hope to do," I told teachers when our conversations took that path, "is more than what teachers have been asked or expected to do. It's an addition to what the children are receiving. And it will be most effective if we can work together, and—if you are willing—if you follow up in the classroom and make praying an ordinary thing in their living." Teachers listened. I had the feeling that they would see what they would see.

For this first meeting, I wanted both to capture their attention by doing something which I supposed they were unfamiliar with, and I wanted to get a sense of their attitude toward God. Consequently I did a fantasy with them. This and other phantasies, with methodology, are found in my earlier book: *Imagine That!*.*

"First," I said to the children, "sit where you are, and stretch. Stretch so high that your sides almost hurt. Stretch! Now relax, with a noise. . . . That's not much of a noise! Stretch again. Harder! Harder! Now let your breath out with a noise, and relax. That's better . . . but you can be louder yet. (Did that surprise them! I can do this because, first: It *is* relaxing; and second, we have no classroom as an immediate neighbor, so we disturb no one). For the third time I said: stretch, stretch hard, and relax with a noise." They did. Small laughs were scattered around the room.

"Fine. Now, if you want to, lie down. If you prefer not to, remain sitting." Virtually all of the children chose to lie down. "Make yourselves comfortable." (Inevitably some child will give a large, fake snore). "I suppose most of you are inclined to think that relaxing and going to sleep are the same thing. They can be. But they don't have to be. For what we are going to do, I want you to be relaxed and very, very alert. Good things happen to you when you have that combination: relaxed and very alert.

"Breathe in and out slowly and quietly . . . slowly and quietly. Pay attention only to your breathing for the next minute or two."

I turned the cassette player on. This time I used an environmental tape: an English meadow with birds and insect sounds.

*Marlene Halpin, *Imagine That!* (Dubuque: Wm. C. Brown Company Publishers, 1981).

"Now I want you to imagine yourselves out in the country on a very beautiful day. It is your favorite time of year. The temperature is just right. It's very, very pleasant. You are alone, and you are enjoying that. Look around you in the country on this beautiful day in your favorite season of the year. . . .

"Gently, as in a dream, you are becoming aware that God is appearing to you as a tree. God gradually is appearing to you as a tree. Let the 'God tree' come to you in your imagination. Let it come—it will. . . . Look at your 'God tree'. What does it look like? What is its size . . . shape . . . color? . . . Is anything happening in it or near it?

"Now you are becoming aware that you are a tree. Let it come to you. What kind of tree are you? (To my surprise, the little children—kindergarteners and first graders—would smile; some with intense little faces, started to draw their images in the air). What does your tree look like? How close or far are you from the God tree? Is anything going on in or near you? . . .

"Look around. Are there any other trees in sight? Sometimes there are, sometimes not. If there are, what are they like? . . . Where are they in relation to the 'God tree' and to yours? Is anything going on in or around them?

"Now, something changes. (I say this in a very definite voice). What changes? . . . How does that change affect your tree?"

After a long pause I say: "Let the phantasy fade. Come back to this room, this time, the other children, your teacher and me. Open your eyes. Sit up slowly. Take a moment by yourself. Pay attention to how you are feeling."

I asked the children to sit in groups of four and tell each other as much as they wanted about what happened in their phantasy, repeating the questions for them.

"No one *has to* share their phantasy. If, for any reason at all, you chose not to, just say: 'I pass.' That will be respected. Ordinarily I do want you to tell a few others, because when you hear your own voice say your phantasy, it helps you understand some things about yourself. But if you don't want to, that is O.K. with me. I want you to listen to each other, and don't make comments or ask questions. There will be time for that in a few minutes. Understand?" They said they did, and began to share their phantasies. "Man, that was wierd!". . . "You know happened in mine?". . . "Well, *my God tree* . . ."

Most of the children had the ordinary trees of their experience (sometimes a tree they knew from their home or their grandparents home) as both the God tree and theirs. About half of them had the same kind of tree for the God tree and theirs. A few children saw the tree in our prayer room. Many, many of the little ones saw fruit trees, or trees which were in flower as they are in the spring. Some had seen shiny trees, glowing trees, silver or gold trees. One had purple stripes! ("I like purple.") Unlike adults, many children saw the God tree in a different season from their tree. They used words for the God tree such as, "nice," "big," "pretty," "happy," "strong," "humongous." Usually their tree was close to the God tree; and generally there were other trees around. Some trees were close, some a little distance away, sometimes a few were dead. Some were touching: "The shiny God tree touched me and I began to shine, too." Generally, something was going on, and generally it was predictable: birds, bees, pets or other small animals, bugs, children scampering around or playing. One child had a unicorn; several saw horses. Some had picnics, even complete with barbeque grill and food. Overall the children evidenced being ordinary, happy children. They had a sense of fun and a little wonder, and they felt good about God.

Beginning with the third grader's responses to the "What changes?" question more attention was needed there than to any other part of the phantasy.

"It rained," one child reported. "It was a hot day, so the tree roots took in the water and it felt good." "Which trees?" I asked. "*All* of them!" was the quick answer—given with a look that indicated that I was less than intelligent.

As with adults (with whom I had used this phantasy many times) changes included storms, wind, changing seasons, snow, night time, lightning, and rain. More children than adults, however, said things like: "I was hit by a car;" "I was nearly bumped into;" "I was chopped down;" "My brother broke a twig off my tree."

"Chopped down" came often through the upper and middle grades. "What happened when your tree was chopped down?". . . A shrug. "I don't know."

"Well, your phantasy isn't finished yet, and that's O.K., because I didn't give you time for that. Let's take the time now. Go back into your phantasy and tell me what happened after your tree was chopped down."

"They made a fire with it and all that is left is ashes.". . . "They throw it into the garbage.". . . "They are building a house with it.". . . "Kids are making a tree house with it."

"That's fine," I encouraged them, "but your phantasy still isn't finished. Something will happen. Watch, and tell me when it does."

Almost always (and more to my initial surprise than theirs) the God tree comes over and touches them. ("Trees can't walk! But the God tree, full of blossoms and cherries at the same time, came over. It's weird!") "The God tree touches me; I grow again and feel happy." Jimmy, a third grader, experienced a surprisingly complete sequence. He reported that both God and he were Christmas trees, chopped down, brought to a home, decorated, and enjoyed at Christmas.

"After Christmas," Jimmy said, "they undecorated us, threw us into the fireplace and burned us up." He was smiling.

"Then what?"

"Oh, our ashes went up the chimney, down onto the snow, and we grew into new trees!"

Over and over again death is followed by resurrection in the young children's phantasies. In *every* instance when the tree had been chopped down the child saw the tree growing again. Most times the God tree came over; with the junior high students the God tree came part of the way, and their tree stump had to go part of the way, and then the God tree touched their stump back into life and growth. Junior high students are developing in their sense of responsibility for their lives. Little ones are incapable of this yet. Their developmental stages showed clearly in their phantasies.

Al, a seventh grader saw "all kinds of spirits coming from the God tree. It was wonderful!" He said with a wondering face. A fifth grader also saw spirits coming from the God tree. "They kind of rested in my tree and made me happy," Hugh said. "Then kids came and climbed my tree and I was happy." Anna, a eighth grader, changed her tree to the beach with wind, wave, storms. "I loved it!" A second grader announced, "me and God fed the squirrels."

A surprising number (to me) of junior high students had very "scary and lonely" reactions to: "What changed?" What changed was that all of the other trees disappeared. So did the birds and small animals. What the youngsters said, in desolate voices, was: "I was left all alone.". . . "The other trees all disappeared.". . . "Nothing else was in sight."

"I was left all alone." Too many said that for any other child to do anything but sympathize. There, too, I encouraged them to go back into the phantasy. They were more reluctant to do so than the chopped down ones. I urged them to do it. Mostly with small sighs they complied.

"See your tree all alone," I reminded them. "Then, look again. Something else will change. Let it happen, then tell me."

Sometimes another tree or two came back at a distance. More often it was the God tree they saw. Ordinarily, the God tree came toward them, then stopped. "Why does it stop?"

"What's the matter with your tree meeting the God tree?" Frowns disappeared. "It's O.K.!" Voices picked up on the second time they said, "It's O.K.! It's O.K.!"

Children of all ages saw themselves as blossoming trees, or trees heavy with fruit—mostly apples or cherries, a few pears or peaches. They liked that; they liked it less when people came and picked their fruit. A few became frightened when *all* their fruit was taken. Sue, a seventh grader, said, "I said they could have some, but they took it all!" "What might that mean to you? What might you want to do about that in your own life?" Sue became very thoughtful.

Classroom teachers agreed to pursue this in their own classrooms. It was obvious that these older children were growing past the nice stage of *talking* about sharing and caring, and beginning to understand the cost of this aspect of being Christian.

"Scary" was used to describe the fright of being left alone; "scary" was used, also, to describe *awe*. Eddie, a sixth grader, said: "My God tree came on fire. It was scary, but I liked it and I was happy."

More than one of the grades had children who reported, "The God tree grew, and my tree grew too." In subsequent prayer room sessions, children returned spontaneously to their tree phantasy. Almost always it was to report growth of their tree.

Johnny, another sixth grader, looked at me quietly for a few minutes, and then asked: "Things changed fast in my phantasy. Will they change as fast in my real life?"

"Sometimes it might seem that way. Do you go out for any sport?"

"Football."

"Do you think it would be a fast change from where you are now, to playing football in one of the major leagues?"

"Fast! No! I have to get taller and heavier and practice a lot before I think about that."

"Right! But even now, when the coach pulls out the playbook, and explains a new play, and you try it, what happens?"

"We make mistakes, then we catch on, then it works real good."

"Right again! I think if you watch your life—and to watch it with God is a way of praying—you'll make some mistakes, you'll catch on, and your life will work well. It generally does not happen fast."

"That's enough for now. I would guess, that if you really did this phantasy, you'll find parts of it coming back to you during the next few days. When it does, simply ask yourself: 'What might it mean?' and pay attention to the answer, and what you might want to do about it, if anything. O.K.?" It seemed O.K.

After another stretch (let out with a noise—they became noisier faster this time) I again invited them to relax and to stay alert.

"We know God is always present, always with us. Why don't you invite God into your heart? And when He comes, give Him a tour of your heart. Show Him whatever you want, even those secret places you usually don't show anybody, or talk about.". . .

"Now show God your tree and your God tree and show him how you see Him. Remember, you said things like 'Big, strong, nice, happy, protecting.' But now use only the words that describe *your* tree. If you don't want to use words, just show Him how you see Him. He understands. . . .

"Put into your heart all the people who love you and all the people you love. You and God look at them, and love them together. If anything special or different is going on with any of them—like someone's birthday or anniversary, or if your mom made you something special, or something your dad talked to you about, anything at all—let God know it from you . . . and then you and God love those special people together.

"You and God keep on loving your special people but let them fade now and you be alone with God. You just told Him how you see Him. Let God tell you now how much He loves you. Let yourself *enjoy* God's loving you."

Jenny, with a dimple in her chin, opened her blue eyes slowly as she gestured for me to come closer. "I think I hear Him," she whispered.

"Good," I said. "*Enjoy* being with God."

The little ones smile, wiggle, and at the end, wave goodbye to God silently. Middle grades and older children become very quiet. "I never thought about talking to God like this," commented Tim. "I like it." Other eighth graders agreed.

After the quiet time I asked them to open their eyes slowly and sit up slowly. "Spend a moment by yourself," I invited them. And then: "Let's end by praying together the prayer that Jesus taught us to pray: Our Father. . . ." They do join in the prayer, but in remarkably subdued voices.

Later one of the teachers, Shirley, told me that one of the little boys in her class said all he could see in his imagination was "colors," and was that all right? Shirley had assured him that it was, and they talked about the colors he liked that he saw for God and himself.

I told the children who had begun to be more lively in the prayer room than I wanted: "This is a prayer room, not a play room. It is a happy place and a room to enjoy, but not a room to play in." Evidently, this struck one of the first graders. I met Jackie in the hall on his way to the boy's room. He moved up close to me, looked up, and said: "It's not a pway woom. It's a pway woom, Wight?"

"Right!"

In Summary

Praying

What's important for a milkstool is that its three legs are of equal length.

What's important for praying is that we pray in three different ways:

1. praying alone, with God in our heart
2. praying with a few other people, whom we know (family, class)
3. praying in church with many people, according to the rites and rituals of the Church

Praying Alone with God

1. any time
2. any place
3. for however long (or short) you want
4. in any way (words, feelings, music, dancing, just being to-gether)

However we pray with God in our heart—we cannot make a mistake!

Be Aware

God is always with us,

God likes having us with Him.

It's fine to "do a lot of nothing" together with God,

as we do with other persons

whom we love, and
who love us.

Chapter 4

More Prettier

(Who Knows You, and Who Loves You?)

You never know what's going to come from what—especially with children. In October some of the teachers were telling me that there was a good deal of teasing going on. Some of it was the usual boy/girl thing, especially in the upper grades. Some of it in the middle grades was beginning to get ugly on an interracial basis. Teachers were handling it in the classroom, of course. But might we deal with it in the prayer room?

When the children came in for their second session in the prayer room, I greeted them with a tape of Galway playing *Stamitz*. After they had a pillow and were settled, I put this question to them: "Who, in all the world, knows you best?"

The answers were expectable. Parents, grandparents (with the sweetest smiles when they said, "my grandma, my grandpa)", assorted relatives, God, Jesus, teachers, yourself. The little ones often included pets; the older ones, their best friends.

The second question was "Who, in all the world, loves you best?"

The answers were expectable. Parents, grandparents (the sweetest smile when they said "my grandma, my grandpa)" assorted relatives, God, Jesus, teacher, yourself. The little ones often included pets; the older ones, their best friends.

I asked them to think about what they had just said. It didn't take long for them to put it together: they were naming the same people for both questions.

"Why might that be?" I asked them.

"Well," Lisa said, "we're around each other a lot, so we really know each other."

"Yeah," Jimmy added, "It's like they sort of know what you mean even when it doesn't come out right."

"That's because you're close by most of the time," Tom said.

"True," I responded. "Let me ask you almost the same thing from another point of view. How many of you have had the experience of someone not liking you? Not wanting to play with you?"

Kindergarten and first grade children looked puzzled. None of them raised hands, except the teacher and me. By the third grade hands were becoming plentiful; by sixth, every hand in the room was raised.

"That's pretty normal," I told them. "Now I want you to close your eyes for a moment, and let yourself remember what it *feels* like when you know someone does not like you. . . . Are you willing to say one feeling out loud?"

Most of the classes had very verbal children. "I feel left out.". . . "I feel like, like—you know—like I'm not as good as the other kids.". . . "I get mad!". . . "I get lonely.". . . "I feel empty.". . . "I'm sad, even now when I think about it.". . . By seventh grade the terms were intensifying to, "You wonder what you did wrong.". . . "I feel guilty, but I really don't know why.". . . "I get unsure, and—you know what? I feel like somebody bruised me.". . . "I guess I feel worthless.". . . "I'm sad.". . . "I'm hurt."

For a while the eighth graders were very silent. When no one admitted to having been disliked, I thought a moment, and then I said: "Please, everyone close your eyes. On your honor, will you keep your eyes closed until I say to open them?" Heads nodded affirmatively. "Now," I continued, "with everyone's eyes being closed except mine, how many of you have had the experience of being disliked?" One hundred percent of the hands shot up. "Thank you. Please put your hands down. Now open your eyes."

"You have a right to privacy, and you need never share anything in this room which you do not want to share. On the other hand, if you do decide to share, you are being generous with each other in a way that can be helpful to everyone including yourself. Are you willing to say out loud why it is that you find it so difficult to talk about yourselves and your own real experiences? I know it is not for lack of something to say. What is it that holds you back?"

Two answers came with the most frequency:

"I'm afraid of saying something wrong."

"I'm afraid I'm the only one thinking that, and the other kids will laugh or think I'm weird, or something."

We talked a bit about the possibility of saying something wrong—in point of fact, unless God moves over and gives up His being God to you, saying something wrong is to be expected. And yes, you might be the only one thinking that, and you might not. Either way it could be good; either way it could be bad. How will you ever know if you don't try it? And yes, the other kids might laugh, or might think you are weird, and that is hard to have happen to you. By the way, why do kids laugh at one another?

"Because it's funny.". . . "Because I get embarrassed and I don't know what to do.". . . "Because I don't like the other kid, anyway.". . . "Because the other kids laugh, and that makes me laugh.". . . "I don't know—I just do."

"Look at what the class has just said," I encouraged them. "How much of it has to do with how well the other person knows you?"

We pushed that around for awhile. Our conclusion was that, junior high is like that: some of it is fun, some of it is very uncertain. There are things to enjoy in junior high—as during any age period—and things to suffer through, and learn from, and gradually one becomes the kind of human being one wants to be.

"You have every right to make choices," I told them. "That's part of the freedom God gives all human beings. What I want to encourage you to do is to look at your choices—at the pluses and minuses in whatever you decide to do—and do the best you are able to that day. Part of doing your best—if it is something of significance—is to talk it over with someone who knows you and whom you can trust to give an honest opinion. Part of doing your best is to imagine the consequences of your decision, and to put into your decision whether or not living the result is worth it to you. And part of your decision is to go over it with God quietly and wait to see if some other ideas come to you.

"The thing of it is," I added, "this is the way it will be all during your life. No matter what age you are, you have to make decisions. You can only do what you can do that day. And that is good enough, provided you do think not only of your decision, but of it's implications for yourself and for others, and are as honest as you are able to be in God's presence. You will probably make some mistakes, but they needn't be sinful mistakes."

The children were listening. I knew I'd come back to this more than once, so we moved on to the people who know us and love us.

All of the fourth graders had said they knew somebody who didn't love them all of the time. These children used the word "miserable" more than the others; "left out," and "hurt," were used frequently also. Tommy said, "Another boy wanted to fight with me. I didn't want to become enemies, so I didn't. Then he called me bad names." And when Jerry voiced, "I get very scared. What if nobody you meet ever again likes you?" Many little heads were shaking up and down.

This group seemed, somehow, more sober than the others. I wondered what was going on inside those nine-year-old heads. So I questioned: "When I said that generally the people who know you best love you best, no one disagreed with me out loud. I'm not sure you are agreeing with me, either. Is someone willing to tell me how you feel about this?"

After a moment's silence Ann's hesitant voice could be heard: "I think God always knows us best, and God always loves us best."

"I do too," I answered her. "What about people in your family?"

"My grandma does," she said with a tremulous and sweet smile.

"And my grandpa." This response came from Franky.

Finally, Rosemary broke through for the class. "What about when your parents get divorced?"

"What about it?"

"Well, they're supposed to know you best and love you best, and . . . and . . . I feel left out."

"Me, too," David said slowly. "I feel like it's my fault, and I keep on doing what I can do different."

"I tried to fix it," Cathy said, "but I couldn't. Now I live with my second dad. . . . My real dad only called me once in my whole life after him and my mom got divorced." Her eyes filled with tears.

I saw the teacher start. Motioning her closer, I asked if she wanted to help us in the discussion. Shirley moved over toward Cathy.

"We talked about this before, Cathy." Cathy and the other children acknowledged that they had. "And we talked about how grownups, no different from children, don't always know how to handle things well. Maybe your dad loves you so much that he does not know how to handle the situation. It can't be easy for him not living with you and your brother, and not being with you as you grow up. Maybe he misses not living with you so much that he does not know how to talk to you."

The children listened like sponges, not denying the maybe, but not being convinced either.

"But if they know each other, how come they don't love each other anymore? And if they don't love each other anymore, will they stop loving me?"

"We don't know if they don't love each other any more," their teacher said to them. "What we do know is that they decided they don't love each other the way a husband and wife do to make a good marriage. They think they made a mistake and have to fix it even though it is very painful for them and for you. But you are forever their children, and their love for you can go on even if they are not married to each other any more."

"I go to a counselor." Once Johnny said it, three others raised hands and simultaneously called out, "Me, too!" Johnny continued, "My counselor gave me a book about divorce." He stopped.

"What did you like best about the book?"

"It says that divorce is not the kid's fault."

"Do you believe it?"

". . . sort of."

"My therapist says the same thing."

I turned to the other two children. "What about your counselors?"

"Mine says it, too," "Mine too."

"Well, that's four out of four. Do you believe your counselors?"

Most unenthusiastic affirmative answers were given by the children.

Sam injected, "I think my mom and dad are getting divorced. He doesn't come home, and she says he has to work. But my mom cries alot. She even cries when she tells me Dad has to work. I wish they'd tell me."

"It's really hard being uncertain, isn't it?"

"Yes." His big brown eyes wandered out to space. He took his thumb out of his mouth just long enough to say, "My mom fixes things around the house all the time. Why can't she fix this?"

We spent a little more time encouraging and comforting the children (it so happened that ten of the nineteen children in the room have divorced parents). Shirley indicated she'd continue the follow up with her class, and we continued with the prayer experience.

"When we pray," I said to these very subdued children, "we bring ourselves and whatever is going on in our lives to God. We show Him, tell Him, and ask Him whatever it is that comes in our everyday living. Before we start praying that way, let's look at some slides and see what they might mean to us."

I put Beethoven's *Pastorale* into the cassette player, and turned the slide projector on. Generally, I try to find something very ordinary to express what we had been discussing, and take pains to photograph it well. For this session I used dandelions. The first slide was of a vacant lot, unkept, overgrown, and scattered with dandelions.

"Ugh! Weeds!" is the first reaction. "My dad doesn't like dandelions on our lawn. Our next door neighbor came over last year and yelled at my mom and dad because we had dandelions on our lawn."

"Well, a lot of people think of them as weeds, and many people want their lawns to be all green. And if they want all green lawns, that's O.K. Let's look at the dandelions themselves for awhile."

Progressive slides began to show the dandelions closer and closer, until one flower filled the frame. Color is lovely. Thread-like petals fill out into full bloom.

"Oh, they are more prettier!" a voice calls out. "I like them better!"

"Oh, but they are the same flowers as in the first slides. They are not prettier. *We* are closer. . . . They seem bigger and more beautiful."

"The closer we get to people, do you think they are prettier?"

Several of the children moved very close to each other and began to look at each other bug-eyed, and to giggle.

"What do you think gets prettier as we get closer? What is the most beautiful thing about a person?"

It took a few attempts, but they finally got to saying things like, "your heart," "what you're like inside," "the love you feel."

"Do you think most people are beautiful inside?"

We agreed that they are, but we don't always get to know everyone that well. If we did, we would probably love most people very much.

Then the images on the slides begin to change. Dandelions live and die, and when the flower dies there comes the puffy balls of seeds. As I pictured a large group of dandelion seed heads, another "ugh" was elicited. In the kindergarten one of the children ran up to the wall and blew on the seeds. The camera closed in until one great puff filled the wall. "Oh!"

"Look at it," I urged them. "Look at how beautiful it is. Look at one seed."

I went to the image on the wall and touched the center of a seed. "For it to stay in place it needs six other seeds. Count them." While I kept a finger on a center seed and touched the ones that touched it, they counted: "One, two, three, four, five, six." Willie, a farmer's little boy, pronounced bravely, "If it doesn't stay in place long enough to . . . to mature, when you plant it, it won't grow."

"What do you think that might mean for us?"

"We have to stay in place until we grow?". . . "We need other people around us.". . . "We need to help each other.". . . "No one makes it alone.". . . "It's nice to have friends . . . and family."

The next slide showed the head of the seed from underneath. "Look how strong, how individual each seed is." I directed them. Successive slides were of closeups of individual seeds. After the "ohs" and "ahs" we talked about what the dandelions might be telling us.

"Well, we need to stick together, but we have to be strong in ourselves.". . . "Each one of us is a separate person.". . . "I have to be my own person."

"What do you think lets each of us, as strong and independent as we might be, stick together?" Looking at the closeup of the seeds, the tacky fibers are visible. "Skin and bones," ventured a little one. "Well, they hold us together inside. "What helps us to be together outside?" "Hands.". . . "Holding hands.". . . "Loving each other.". . . "Caring for each other.". . . "Sharing what we have."

The next slide showed the strength of each individual seed; it also showed that every seed is connected to a strong stem. Everybody looked at that. "My, they are all connected!" The older children exclaimed, "They're united with one base."

"Yes! What might that mean for us?" The children moved easily into the notion of being connected with God. No matter how strong we are, no matter the six (or so) other people we touch so that we all stay in place and grow, we still need to be connected with God and to be ourselves. "What's the strongest connection?" "To the stem." "What's our strongest connection?" "To God." "Does anyone have any more ideas as we look at these last slides?" Junior high students said clearly: "I have to be my own person. But I can't be my own person alone. Only, sometimes, I think I make touching others more important than being connected to the stem. . . ."

"They all are important, aren't they?"

"Yes."

"But it's a good thing to know what is the most important. Other people can make a mistake about you, or can change their minds—for whatever reason or depending on what they are going through in their own lives. But God never makes a mistake. The Scriptures tell us that after God made us, He looked at what He had made, and saw that it was very good. What we can always count on is that God made us good, God does not make mistakes, and God always knows us and loves us best. You can count on that, your whole life long."

The class was ready for their quiet time with God. I changed the tape to Steve Halprin's tape *Spectrum Suite,* the *Dawn* section. The shades were drawn for the slides so the room was as dim as it would get.

"Make yourselves as comfortable as you want," I invited the children. "Stay alert, and be sure that you all have your own space. If you decide you don't want to pray, that is all right. Just make sure you do not treat any of your classmates unfairly by interfering with their quiet time with God."

The children settled in rather quickly and quietly. Most lay on the floor, heads on big pillows. Some lounged against the wall. Two or three knelt with head in knees. All were very still.

"Welcome God into your heart. He is always present. We need to make ourselves aware that He is with us, loving us. . . . Give Him a tour of your heart. Yes, He does know what is going on with you, but it is good that you tell Him for yourself. You can tell Him anyway you want: use words, or feeling, or just be with Him. Show Him what your heart looks like. If your heart is happy, show Him a happy heart. If your heart is feeling miserable and left out, show Him a miserable and left out heart. If your heart is feeling not sure, show Him an unsure heart. All we ever have for God is the way we are—and that is enough. Show Him the way you are."

After a few minutes (and some tears were leaking down a few little cheeks), "You just looked at dandelions from far away, and then closeup. You saw how beautiful they are, up close. Well, God is up close to your heart. Let Him see how beautiful your heart really is. Whether it is a happy heart or a hurting heart, it is a beautiful heart."

Two or three minutes later, I suggested: "Put into your heart all the people who love you, and all the people you love. Even if you are afraid some might not love you as much as they used to, put them into your heart. . . . Then you and God look at them to-gether. Let Him know what's happening: what's happy, whose birthday it might be, if another baby is on the way, whatever is going on. And if, in your family, you are afraid, or feeling that you should fix things, or make things different, let God know about that from you. Then you and God love these people together."

After allowing several more minutes of quiet I began: "You know God knows you best and loves you best. You can always count on that. If there is a hurt place in your heart, show Him, and ask Him to heal it and to bless you. . . . Then, remembering that God al-ways delights in being with you because He made you and He made you good, and He never makes a mistake, take a few moments to *enjoy* God's loving you."

We ended as usual. First I asked them to open their eyes, and then, to sit up gently. It takes a little time for children (of any age) to disengage from prayer that intimate and that intense. When they seemed about ready, we prayer the prayer that Jesus taught us to pray, remembering ourselves, parents, and all those we touch and who touch us.

Several days later Jim, the seventh grade teacher, stopped by my office. He told me of the follow-up he had done with his class.

"Symbolism has always interested me," he said, "so I explained symbolism to the kids. They have a hard time seeing that there can be different right answers, and symbolism lets you get into that. They feel safer if there is a uniform right answer, and then they get afraid to say what they think it is, for fear that the others will laugh."

Jim went on to say that he and his seventh graders talked about the dandelions. "The puff balls, no matter how pretty they are, are dead. They are dead dandelions." From there he and the class went on to the sequence of death and resurrection in each of our lives . . . how we have to die and be born again. Seeds are good symbols because they create anew, forming themselves over and over.

That group spoke about the different ways we die: physical death, the death that comes from separations like divorce or ending friendships, the death to things in our lives which are good, but which we outgrow; and the death to things in our lives which get in the way of living well: sin.

"The kids look forward to coming back" Jim told me, "and to seeing what they could do with the next symbols you use. You will use more?"

"I sure will!"

There was one more bit of feedback that day. A part-time secretary came in to say how much her little girl loves these special pillows. "But," she quoted the youngster's having told her, "I like the prayer room best because that's where we get to talk to God, and ask Him to come into our heart . . . and He does."

In Summary

From the Dandelion

- The closer we get, the prettier it looks to us.
- The more people really know us (and we, them), the more they are likely to love us (and we, them).

From the Dandelion Seeds—The Silvery Puff Balls

1. One seed in the ball touches six others. We need to be in touch with other people, and they with us. We don't live well alone.
2. Each seed is strong, well-structured and interdependent; we each need to be our own person.

3. Each seed is connected with the stem. We need to be rooted in Christ.

   The seeds come from dead dandelions. The seeds can become alive flowers.

   We can become alive again after each of the deaths in our lives: the things we outgrow or lose; broken friendship or divorce; things we hoped for which did not happen.

Be Aware

All that we have for God in our prayer today,
is
how we are today.

That always
is
enough.

Chapter 5

Why Should I?

(Pray, That Is)

"It's time for another visit to the prayer room," I wrote in a circular note to all the teachers. "Please sign up for a time convenient for your schedule. It will be a pleasure to have you and the children return to the prayer room."

This note was clipped to a schedule covering a two week period in the fall, and indicated time slots when I'd be able to take the children in the prayer room. Teachers always remained with the children in the room. I wanted them there, basically because I think it is a good thing for the children to see two adults taking prayer seriously. Teachers like it because they like the quiet time also and because, "It lets me see the children in another light." Sometimes teachers have become crucial to the discussion—as the day one class began to talk about divorce.

Teachers pick the time slot for their own scheduling convenience. I began hearing different reasons for their selections. "Well," said Marcie, the reason why I try for the 8:30 a.m. period is that then they start the day well. I've noticed they are kinder to each other the days they have been to the prayer room. It lasts. I try to get my eighth graders there first."

Another teacher picks the last session of the day. "I like to send them home happy."

I began this session, after greeting the children and welcoming them, by asking if they had any questions. Some of the youngest ones reported that they asked God into their hearts, even when they were home. One little girl said, "I asked God into my heart when my mother went to bring my sister home from her violin lesson." The children say God comes when they invite Him into their heart.

"Do you like it?"

"Oh, yes!"

"I'm glad." I am not always sure what they mean when they say, "God comes into my heart." But I know I will not make a fuss over it, nor will I ask them to articulate more than they spontaneously do. Children (of any age), I believe, know more than they know they know. Trying to verbalize everything can trivialize some sacred experiences. Language is inadequate for much of prayer: do not some of the mystical writers resort to imagery and poetry to approximate verbally their experiences of God? It is enough that these children are aware of a loving God's presence and have some conscious experience which is affirming to them. I encourage them to continue to invite God into their heart, show Him what is there, love people together, and enjoy His loving them. Or I ask them to engage in any part of the prayer activity depending on how their life is being lived that day.

Joanne, a seventh grader, asked: "Why do my eyes feel glued shut, and my body feel asleep, but my mind is very active? I don't understand it."

"When you concentrate very hard on something, and keep the concentration in a relaxed way, you can feel this way rather easily. Probably your brain waves are on another level. You are not asleep, but you are not very aware of anything going on around you. You are very alive, very concentrated on one thing. Athletes, scholars, and saints have that in common: real, involved concentration. Do you find it pleasing?"

"Yes," Joanne continued, "but—peculiar."

Neal, an eighth grader, took a deep breath as his hand jabbed into the air.

"Neal?"

"I do this stuff at home. I like it when I do it. Then later I think: What am I wasting my time on this for? It doesn't make any sense! Why should I keep it up?"

This is a good question; and one right for 1984. Why should he—or anyone—keep it up?

"You've hit a nail right on the head," I told him. We went on to talk about our culture.

Neal's question hits a deep level. Our educational system takes children and prepares them for coping with a highly complex, technological civilization. Prayer is simple. Perhaps that is why young children, so fresh from the hand of God, can turn around to the simplicity they left so shortly before. Perhaps that it is why older people, educated out of simplicity, have a longer road back. Perhaps that is part of why children respond so happily. Neal is growing up. Implicitly at least he is aware of productivity. We talked about faith and productivity in that room that day.

Probably nothing is more anti-cultural than prayer. What are we educating for? Productivity. "What do you *do?*" is a question readily asked of a new acquaintance. In school, work has to be done. At home, work has to be done. At work, work has to be done. In any organization, work has to be done. We need to have something to show what we have done.

Not so in prayer. In prayer we are with God. That is enough. We do not produce anything. Nor are we graded. There is no way to compete, be rated, or have a score which is better or worse than another person. There is not even a way to compete with ourselves and surpass our own past performance. That is anti-cultural! We have nothing to show for it—in a tangible, immediate sense.

Jesus said, "By their fruits you shall know them." What is the fruit of prayer? That does show—over a lifetime. I doubt that anyone can prove we are more compassionate, more sensitive to other peoples' needs, more generous, more willing to give up comforting but self-destructive behavior, because of our prayer. I think prayer has much to do with the kind of human beings we are—keeping our baptismal vows flourishing. What is rewarded in school and other societies? Achievement, productivity, winning. In prayer? The question is irrelevant. No one even knows who prays, or how, unless an honest and intimate conversation would indicate that.

"So, Neal, your question, I think, comes from our culture: school, T.V., sports—whatever you come into contact with and which has an impact on you. But your question goes further yet."

"Do you believe in God? Do you want to believe in God? If you say "yes" then praying makes sense. If you say "no" then praying is a waste of time and energy.

"For those who believe in God, it is important to have an ongoing relationship. If we believe we come from God and are returning to God, we need to stay in communication. If we believe

God created us, it is important to hear *from Him* what best will give us happy, satisfying, good lives. That's what prayer helps us to do.

"For those who do not believe in God—or do not want to, praying makes no sense. Why spend time and energy trying to communicate with nobody?

"When you begin to pray regularly and with seriousness, you might feel foolish or uncertain. I'd expect that. It's new to you, at least in this way. You might not yet know many people who pray like this—chances are you know some, but they might not talk about it readily. It certainly is not in accord with attitudes found in newspapers, on the soaps, or in the movies.

There is also that pervasive business in our society. People are inclined to say: "Well, I'd like to pray, but I'm so busy." That's true. People are very busy. Perhaps busier than in any other society because we have so many opportunities. Prayer is one of the easiest things to relegate to "when I have time." Unprayed prayer won't show like a frost-heavy refrigerator, a messy bathroom, or unlaundered clothing.

"Neal, you really asked a good question. Probably more than you expected. Let me put it to you as simply and distinctly as I can: Why you should bother to pray ties in with: Do you believe in God? If you do, then pray. Prayer is an irreplaceable dimension of life. Human living is poorer without explicitly being conscious of the God who made us knowingly and lovingly and stays with us all during our life. It is such an abysmal waste not to allow ourselves the pleasure of God's loving company. If you do not believe in God and if you do not want to, then don't pray."

"How do you know?" Neal persists.

Another result of our educational system is showing. For me, education in the United States experienced a water shed in the late 1950's. After Russia's successful launching of Sputnik our country went into a stronger emphasis on math and science. Inductive reasoning received much more attention. Present a rationale. Defend. Prove. Go from hypothesis, to theory, to law. Experiment and prove it. That is appropriate in math and science. God doesn't fit under math and science; God made the things we are trying to understand mathematically and scientifically. And God made us—understanding. Scientific method is well used appropriately in its own area. Scientific method is not appropriate to everything we know.

We don't know all things the same way. I can know you are wearing a pair of Adidas tennis shoes because I can see them and I can read. I don't know how you feel about me quite the same way. Nor can I tell what your relationship to your parents is by looking at your feet. Different areas require different methods. The scientific method does not apply to God.

That brings us the full circuit to faith. "Do you believe? Do you want to believe?" Neal allowed he'd hang in with God. We continued the session.

"The last time you were here," I reminded the children, "we talked about who knows us, who loves us, and how—usually when we get up close—we see how beautiful other people are."

"Like the dandelions!" a little bright voice spoke out.

"Like the dandelions," I continued. "Yes, we need to be strong, to be our own person, as you said the last time. Still we need each other. Today I would like to follow that from two points of view. Ready?"

"Ready!" The children wiggled more comfortably on their pillows.

"First, I'd like to do some more imagining with you—like you did the first time here with the God tree. Do you remember that?" They not only remembered, but a number of children had subsequent reports. Most of them were to the effect that their tree was growing. I'm glad they are aware of it.

"First, take a good hard stretch. Pull your arms up so high that your sides feel it all the way down. Now, relax, breathing out with a noise." This time the children needed no encouragement to let out a breath noisily.

"Tighten up your face, your whole body . . . hold it . . . relax with a noise." They did that, too. "Now lie down, if you wish, or sit comfortably. Be comfortable and relaxed, but very alert."*

"Imagine yourself in some large department store like Gilmores or Jacobsons or (naming local large stores). Go into the store and walk around until you come to the toy department (sporting goods

*This phantasy, too, with methodology, is found in *Imagine That!*, Marlene Halpin (Dubuque: Wm. C. Brown Company Publishers, 1981).

for the upper grades; either works as well in the phantasy). See toys—toys all around. (Five and six year olds emit a spontaneous thin, ready and delightful "OHHHH.") There are toys on the counter, toys on the shelves, toys in the bins, toys all over—everywhere you can see.

"Gently, as in a dream, you feel yourself becoming one of the toys. Let it happen to you in your imagination. What kind of toy do you become?" (I give it a full minute or minute and a half. The youngest children sketch in the air, the toy they are becoming. Most smile slightly; a few frown in concentration.)

"One of the other toys comes over to you to talk with you or maybe play with you. What toy comes to you? Watch, and let it happen."

After a minute or ninety seconds I add a third element: "All of the other toys are watching you and the toy which came over to you. They are watching you, and talking. What are they saying to each other?

"Let the phantasy fade. Come back to this room and the rest of us here. Open your eyes and sit up slowly if you are not sitting already."

I asked the children to break into groups of four, and insofar as they are willing, to tell each other: what toy they became; what toy came to them; what the others were saying (or some piece of sports equipment for the older children). Teachers generally joined a group. The room buzzes with sound. Some children imitate "their" toys. Then we talk about it.

Tops, trunks, E.T. dolls, Barbie dolls were very popular among the younger children. Other dolls came to talk to them. Pac Man and Atari games were named in all grades. T.V. sets, video recorders, robots received attention. "Ugh!" Lee frowned. "I had a computer game, then all the blips began to bleed. I don't like it!"

For Doris, a fourth grader, the other toy wasn't a toy. It was God. "I kept trying to make him a toy, but he stayed God."

"That's all right, Doris. Tell me what the other toys were saying."

"Oh, the toys all liked having God around. It was funny." She paused a moment, wondering at her own next word. "It is funny. When the other toys saw God with me, they all laughed together.

50

I don't know why they laughed, but it was happy. Then God and I laughed, too." She smiled timidly and shrugged.

A sixth grader, with an unusual ethnic first name, was a baseball. A mitt came to talk with him. Some of the other things laughed, called him "fat" and made fun of his name. "Why?" I put to the class, "Why do you think the other sports equipment might react like that to the ball and the mitt?"

"They're jealous. They'd rather be a ball or a mitt than what they are."

"They want to show off."

"They want to look better than the other guy."

"Maybe they think they can get ahead if they put someone else down."

"And what do *you* think?" I pressed them. A few mumbled answers came.

"Maybe they think if they do it to someone else, it won't happen to them."

"I don't know. Kids just do it."

"I guess they're afraid."

"Afraid of what?"

"I think they want to be best friends but are afraid no one will want them, so they laugh and make fun."

Older children were baseballs, basketballs, volleyballs, footballs; baseball bats, tennis racquets, saddles, gold clubs, canoes, tents. Generally the toy (or sports good) which came to them was compatible with them. But what the other toys were saying was important. It shows readily how children (of any age) perceive themselves perceived by others.

Most of them said things like: "May we play with you?". . . "May I come along?". . . "He's the greatest!". . . "I'd like to be with you.". . . "She's the smartest.". . . "Do you want to come to my house?". . . "He's the best!" One thin child said the other toys had been calling out, "Watch out for him! He'll give you a black eye!"

Ray, a fifth grader, had a set and unpleasant expression on his face. I asked him what he was. "I was a soccer ball." Then he blurted out, "No toy came to me. All the other things were laughing, poking each other, and pointing at me. So I fixed them! I just got on the shelf, worked up some speed, and knocked them all down on the floor. Some of them even broke!" There was fire in his eyes and satisfaction in his voice.

"Is that how it is with you?" I asked. He looked sure. "Yes!" "Maybe we can talk about it later. . . . Who else wants to say what the other toys were saying?"

After that class I made sure to see Barbara, the teacher. What's troubling Ray?" I asked her.

"I can't get over it," she replied. "That is exactly what he does with the other children. He doesn't give them a chance to be friendly. He is always picking fights, and he fights hard. The other kids are beginning to avoid him. It's amazing how clear it was in his phantasy."

"Well, things like this do show. How do you see the situation?"

Barb continued, "His parents recently divorced. He's crazy about his dad, but his dad seems to want nothing to do with the boy or his mother. It's affecting him deeply."

Barbara and I talked a bit more. She decided to call the parents and ask them to come for a visit. This is another time I was especially grateful for the classroom teacher's presence. She was there, and she heard the child's reaction to the phantasy. And Barb is in a position to have a follow-up with the boy since he is in her room for the school year.

Some of the older children heard other toys (or sports good) laughing at them—or ignoring them—insults were not uncommon.

"Think a minute," I asked. "Play back the phantasy. Can you put names and faces on the other toys?"

Children are quicker at this than adults. "Sure!" Parents, an aunt, a best friend, and grandparents were named. Mostly other children in the school appeared.

"Don't name the names out loud," I said in a rush. "Just pay attention inside yourself. How might this fit with what we talked about before? When we talked about people who know you and love you best? People who see you up close, like we saw the dandelions?"

Sam said he was a ball. There was only one other ball in the whole store, and the other ball was afraid to come to him. He was afraid because the shelves were full of bats, and the bats looked ready to march on them.

"That's like me," Sally said, "but I think the teasing toys don't really know me."

"Do you want them to?"

"No! . . . I mean . . . maybe . . . I mean, . . . yes, I do!"

"How might you go about it?"

That got into a class discussion about being unsure if other people think like you do or feel like you do, or are they going to laugh?

"It's always the same thing with these children," the teacher and I were agreeing later. "But in each case it is the new and poignant pain of the one suffering it now."

Seventh and eighth graders were preparing for the Sacrament of Confirmation. I did this phantasy with them during their retreat day. The priest present shared his phantasy first. "I was a canoe, and what came to me was a paddle. All the other sports equipment was saying, "Neither one can go any place without the other." And I guess that's right. We don't go anywhere without each other."

I asked the children how many of their images were reciprocal: ball/bat or glove; ball/tennis racket; skis/boots; boat/sail or motor. More than half of the students said that's how it was.

What a natural lead in, on this retreat date, for talking about Saint Paul and what he wrote about people's having different gifts and how together, we make one body. Somehow that epistle made more sense to them in terms of balls and bats, rackets, skis and boats.

For the visuals that day I had worked with the song, "The Rose."* It bothered me that those great lyrics were sung by Bette Midler only at the end of the movie, *The Rose,* while the credits were rolling. The lyrics were most impressive ones to me. Since they are appropriate for the children, especially at the time of Confirmation, I decided to use them.

Consider, if you will, couplets like these:

"It's the heart afraid of breaking that never learns to dance."

"It's the dream afraid of waking that never takes a chance."

We stopped and thought about what things we want so badly we don't let ourselves look at them realistically. Or what it is in our lives that has hurt us so badly that we protect ourselves, and

*"The Rose," by Amanda McBroom. Copyright © 1979 Warner-Tamerlane Publishing Corporation. All rights reserved. Used by permission.

in self-defensiveness stay glum and gloomy—blocking the joy which comes from the presence of God and the Holy Spirit!

"It's the one who won't be taken that cannot seem to give."

There wasn't a youngster in the room who didn't have the experience of having been taken at sometime or another. No one liked it much, either. "Hurtful," I agreed. "There is no need to be naive or stupid or to make of yourself a doormat. That's true. But more important than the fact that you were taken at different times, is: What are you letting it do to you? . . . to your attitudes? . . . to the way you treat other people? What kind of emerging man or woman is that making you?

We talked about mistakes—and learning. We also talked about compassion for ourselves and for others; how difficult—and how satisfying—it is to live a good Christian life. What I enjoyed most was having the pastor and the principal, the teachers and myself, joining together to tell the children that no matter what we adults had thought of or tried, nothing works so well in our lives as trying to follow the way that Jesus taught.

"And the soul afraid of dying that never learns to live."

What fears are real in our lives—fears that might be brought to the Lord for healing, and for us to be strengthened? There is so much fear of being wrong, or different; fear of not being acceptable to other people; fear of not being good enough for—whatever happens to be important to the youngster. Larger fears were mentioned: their parents' marriage—and what will become of them after the divorce; fears of nuclear war, of polluted waters, of environmental depletions. All of these were acknowledged. Then we brought them to prayer.

After a break I invited all those present to be as comfortable as they could in those chairs. (This group was too large for the prayer room.)

"Ask God to come into your heart. After this past hour your heart is probably very full. Give God a tour—show Him the things which are concerning you, how you feel about how other people react to you, what you are afraid of, where you've been abused, what you're afraid to take a chance on, what is it in your life that limits you unnecessarily, how you might help with the large world issues of hunger or pollution or war? Show it all to your God. . . ." (Wait a minute or two.)

"Now, quietly with God in your heart, let one—just one—of those things in your collections come to your awareness. Let it be the most important concern for you this day. Just one thing. . . . Look at that one concern together with God. What do you want to say to Him about it? . . . or ask? . . . or communicate in some way—even if you feel miserable looking at it, or afraid, or uncertain, or angry—however that issue makes you, let God know from you. . . .

"Now be quiet. Just *be* with God. Perhaps He will allow you to understand something, if you are willing; perhaps just being with Him is all you need at the moment. Remember, God is God; God loves you dearly; so take a few moments to rest and enjoy God loving you."

At the end of the six or seven quiet minutes we pray together the prayer that Jesus taught us to pray: That prayer takes care of every need we could possibly have.

On the way out Kathy stopped me. "I like to be with God like that," she told me. "But are you sure that's praying? I told my mom about it, and she asked me why we don't say more prayers?" (Other parents also questioned our not "saying prayers.")

"Kathy, do you like praying?"

"Yes."

"What do you like about it?"

"I feel like I'm with God."

I was reminded of St. Teresa of Avila saying, "when given God, enjoy. Don't seek."

"Kathy, stay with God. Enjoy his company. And, yes, I am sure that this is praying."

In Summary

Welcoming Questions

From this session's questions it became evident that:

1. Praying is altogether natural to the younger children.
2. Praying is pleasurable, but questionable, for the older children.

Faith and our society need some attention. Then the need to make a faith choice (or not) has to be faced.

The Rose

From the lyrics of this song or whatever song you choose might come more reflective questions:

1. What is happening to you in your life which is hurtful?
   - What are you letting this do to you in your attitudes and in the way you treat other people?
   - We cannot control all of what happens to us; we can decide how we let it affect our lives.
2. What is happening to you in your life which makes you afraid?
   - What are you doing about it?

Both the hurts and fears:

1. need to be acknowledged to oneself—at least.
2. are well brought before God in trusting prayer for us to receive strength and healing.

Be Aware

Both Hebrew and Christian Scriptures tell us:
"Do not be afraid."

Often we are.

It is a good thing to bring our fears to God
in loving trust.

Chapter 6

What's Your String?

(What Holds the Beads of Your Days' Events Together?)

Before beginning the next session in the prayer room, I asked the children how many remembered to pray in their hearts since their last visit to the prayer room. One-third to one-half of the children said yes, they had. I reminded them that when they pray like this I'd expect them to have some questions. Did any of them?

George, a fifth grader, said: "I don't really have a question, I just want to say something. Sometimes when God talks to me, I know what He is going to say before He says it." George has brought that up several times since. He does not understand it, it doesn't upset him; it seems always to puzzle him that this happens to him.

Howard, another fifth grader, was the first to ask this question: "When I've invited God into my heart, and He comes, and I show Him things, how do I know if it is God talking to me or my own brain talking to itself?" Howard, as I said, was first. Since that November day, at least one child in every grade from fourth through senior high school asked the same question. *"How do I know if it is God Who is speaking to me, or my own brain?"*

I was surprised. Endless adults of my experience have asked the same question. Theories abound regarding how God comes to us in the depths of our being. Religious psychologists don't question the fact of God's doing so. Like most things with God, however, there is that very real element of mystery—of immanence and of transcendence. In their own direct way the children were demonstrating this again. They had no question that, at times, God did communicate with them. Their question always was one of distinction: was it God, or was it their own inner self? Whose spirit was speaking?

My surprise was not at the question, but at the age of the children asking it. It began with nine year olds and went through every grade level. How seriously we need to take children, I thought. Then I remembered an article I had read on possible space colonization. Looking forward toward it, a futuristic organization polled its members. The gist of the principal question was this: given humanity's possibility of starting all over again in space, which of earth's mistakes might be avoided? Two answers headed the list of responses: religion and marriage.

I spoke about this article with a friend who is a psychologist. Don's immediate comment was, "Of course! Those are the two most demanding situations in a person's life!" Most demanding in the commitment they entail: both involve our whole selves; both are life-long in intent.

That religious inclinations, thoughts, and feelings are evident in the child is no surprise. Their depth needs validation and affirmation. I find that children are not looking for endless theology. There is a real limit to what they (we!) can understand. What is wanted is the forum to speak of these things, have them received and affirmed. Their experiences will multiply so nurtured.

I thought of John's concern for the young people who are leaving the Church. "I don't get anything out of it," is the common cry. Perhaps that says that the expectation of Church is to give us religion, that we put it on from the outside, that it somehow is something we "do" and that makes us "religious." What was happening over and over with the children was that we were seeing their spiritual life emerging articulately with tentative questions. But the questions themselves showed a real, and unquestioned, *experience*. What they were asking, I think, was how to fit this experience into the rest of what they were learning. Or, as in Howard's case, how to tell the difference?

"That is such an important question," I said to Howard, "that we need to give it some attention. I want you to think about it and see how far you can go with it by yourself. After you have thought a while, will you come back? Then we will talk about it together." Howard was not enthusiastic about the proposal, but he agreed.

Time passed quickly. On and off I wondered where Howard was, but somehow did not go looking for him. About three weeks later, after a session with his class, Howard lingered after the other children. "I think I have it figured out," he told me with the utmost seriousness and gentle confidence.

"Do you? Will you tell me what you came to?"

That little boy stood there, feet apart, a wisp of blonde hair straggling into his eyes, and slowly said: "I think that when I've been watching TV or out playing ball and then go and get quiet and invite God into my heart, then I think that my own brain is talking to itself. But when I get . . .", he shifted slightly, groping for the right words, "when I get . . . empty . . . empty like an empty piece of paper, then I think it is God talking to me."

He stood there looking at me with the utmost gentleness and conviction. Never in my life have I heard it put so directly and so well.

"Howard, I think you are right. Thank you for taking your question seriously, and for paying attention to what is going on inside of you. I hope you keep doing that. Tell me, do you find it hard to get empty?"

"Sometimes," he said. "Sometimes it takes a lot of time, and my mom calls me to do things."

"Yes, that happens. But we still need to make time to be empty for God." He nodded in agreement and slowly rejoined his classmates.

How simple. How simple it is to pray and to affirm the praying experiences of others. How is it that we, some of us, get so caught up in the notion of privacy, or that that sort of thing is only for great saints—none of whom I expect to know (unless I read about them somewhere, or there's a television special on them). How is it that we fail to take our Baptism seriously, or the other sacraments which nourish us from within? Jesus said he came to bring life, and life abundant. (John 10:10) Children feel the stirrings of that life. They need to be affirmed.

Affirmation has another requirement, too. It is called time. We in our society are so busy. There are demands on our energy, on our time—demands which never seem to stop. Because we have so much at our disposal, we have often been talked into doing too much. Where is the time to "get empty?" Howard said it so well. After TV, after playing ball, "I think it is my own brain talking to itself." It takes time to get empty, so we can consciously receive God. Affirming the inclination toward God is important. Children need more than encouragement. How can we model for our children the importance of this—by giving it time ahead of other things? There's an old proverb: "actions speak louder than words." How do our actions demonstrate God's importance in our lives? Leaving time to go to church on Sunday is good—but not good enough for living life. Where is the time to get empty. If we are convinced of the importance of prayer time, we will make it. As in any good, long-term relationship some prime-time is needed. Not just time tacked on at the end of a day or when some expected activity is cancelled. Prime time for a prime activity—time to get empty. All of us need attention to giving God prime time.

In the prayer room, the class and I went back to the discussion we had about how you know when someone likes you. One of the best ways, according to the children, is "to spend time together doing a lot of nothing." They remembered having said that. Well, that's one of the best ways to pray. To spend time with God doing a lot of nothing is a very good prayer; Howard had found it. Some of the other children had, too.

For this session I began with the question: "How do you wake up in the morning?"

"When my mom calls me.". . . "When the alarm goes off.". . . "When my kid brother pulls my toes.". . . "Gradually. Sometimes I go back to sleep.". . . "My dad won't let me do that!"

"What is the first thing you do after you wake up?"

"God to the bathroom.". . . "Study.". . . "Brush my teeth.". . . "Get dressed.". . . "Get washed.". . . "Look for my socks."

This time in the prayer room I went back to one of the first questions I had asked the children. "When do you pray?" In what special way do you say hello to God? I'll talk more about string in a little bit, but how about asking God's help for the day—blessing us, our family, teachers, all the people we are going to meet—each day?"

"Sometimes I talk to God in the morning—like when I have a math test." "That's good. How about talking to Him *everyday*—just because you're you and God's God?

We paid particular attention to evening prayers. Some of the children say them. Some looked sheepish when I asked. A few looked away or became very interested with fingernails or shoelaces. "Good", I thought, "at least there is some awareness in them about evening prayers. I asked, "Why should we bother praying before we go to bed?" Children gave expectable answers.

"To pray that no one tells on me."

"To thank God for the day."

"To tell God about our troubles."

"To ask God's forgiveness for what we did wrong."

"To pray for someone who's sick."

"To make up for being bad."

"You are all right," I told them, "every one of you. I'd like to spend our time together today talking about another way to pray before going to bed—or anytime you want, but at least once a day. Evening is a good time."

I asked them what their string was? Of course, no one knew what I meant. "Well, what do you use a string for?"

"To tie things together."

"Right! Anything else?"

"Sometimes you can fish with it."

"You can put things on it, like popcorn at Christmas."

"It's good to practice knots with."

"Yes, all of that is true," I told them. "Today what we are going to pay attention to is using a string to string beads. When you were a very young child, did you ever have big wooden or brightly colored plastic beads? Did they come with a sort of a long shoe lace—only it was probably red—that you strung the beads from?"

Most of the children signaled that they had. The older ones smiled, as if now they could hardly believe that once they had been so young. They remembered. The kindergartners remembered best—they, some of them, still had those beads.

"Today we are going to imagine the string as our telling God about the day. The beads are the people we met, the things we did, what happened to us, anything at all that went on in our lives that day. "Does anyone remember how we can tell God things?"

In most classes the children looked puzzled. Then a few began to say brightly, "Like in the prayer room? We can tell God what we want in words . . . or in feelings." "Or we can just *be* with Him!"

"Or we can show Him without saying anything!"

"That is true. The important thing is that we do let Him know, from us. Because God is God, we can let Him know anything we want and we are sure He will understand. So when we string the beads of our day together, we can do it in words, or feelings, or just show Him, or just be with Him letting Him into the day. Letting God know from us is the string. Let's look at what the beads might be. Maybe we can practice by doing today so far, as if it were tonight. "Are you willing?"

They were—with varying degrees of enthusiasm. To the little ones I said, "Pick a color for people. Since people are the most important things in our lives (Aren't they? Oh, they are!), pick your favorite color and we'll use that for people. Kindergartners and first graders tend to say their favorite colors out loud. "Red!". . . "Purple!". . . "Green!". . . "Sister, can I have pink with white polka dots?". . . "Yellow!"

"Have in your imagination round beads and square beads or any shape you want. Pick your favorite colors and put on your string one bead for each person. As you do, tell God about you and that person for today. For instance, let God know about your house this morning. Show Him how it was with your family. Pick a bead for each one, tell Him what it was like, ask Him for whatever you and your family need, and to bless you and all of them.

"Are your family beads on the string? . . . Then who did you meet on the way to school? Maybe you want a bead for the bus driver, and some for the other children on the bus. Who did you sit with? Talk with? How did that go? Let God know about it.

"What was it like when you got to school? Perhaps you'd like to pick a teacher bead, and beads for your classmates."

"That's a whole lot of beads," piped up Martha.

"Yes, it is. Suppose you pick enough beads just for the people you had something to do with directly. Will that cut it down enough?" It would.

Next you might want to think about what happened to you that was special. Maybe it was something funny. Pick a funny color and let God in on the humor of it. "Green," giggled Irene. Maybe it was something ugly, like a fight. Pick an ugly bead and let God know what happened. "Gray. Gray is an ugly color," stated Ben. "Maybe it was having fun. Then take a fun bead to put on your string. Maybe you were mean to someone. Put a bead on and let God know why you were mean, and how you feel about it now."

"When you get all the beads on your string, look them over."
"Do you have to put everything on your string? *Everything?*" The question came from a very serious Francis. He looked a little worried.

"No, not everything. Just those which come to you, which were important to you during the day. Some days your string might be very short. Other days, kind of long. The important thing is that you do go over the day with God, and that you are together with what made you glad, with those that you might want to say, "I'm sorry" to, or perhaps you want to ask for help to do better, or tell God those things you were proud of. Or you can use beads (all in your imagination of course) for people who are important to you, and people who could use some help and you want to remember them to God. You can make the string as long or as short as you want for that day.

"Why should we do it?" sixth grader Karl asked.

"If you believe we come from God and we are going back to God, it is a good thing to stay connected along the way. Spending some time everyday going over the day lets us stay conscious of our own lives. Often times people pick up ways of behaving so slowly, they don't happen to notice. If they are good ways, we ought to enjoy them. If they aren't good for us, if they are going to hurt us in the long run, then we need to be alert to those choices. It's important to be healthy in our spirit as well as in our bodies. So if we are with God every day—going over the day with Him— we are more likely to be the kind of people we want to be, and be happy with ourselves."

Karl thought a minute. "Is that all there is to it?"

"I'm glad you asked. No. Just reviewing the day, however you do it with God in your heart, isn't quite enough. It's a good idea to pray a bit after that."

"How?"

"The way that best suits you—or your day. You might be quiet a moment or so, and let one thing from the day come back to you. Then you and God together could look at that one thing. You could wonder why that one came up; maybe it means something to you. Or if you are uncertain about something, or you don't know what to do, that's a good one to hold before God, letting Him know that you are uncertain. The possibilities are as endless as the people who pray and the things which happen to them during the day. I can't tell you what to pray about. You know for yourself each time. If it's been a ho-hum day, rather boring, nothing special, then that's what you have for God that day. Just pray with whatever it's truly like for you, and make that the stuff of your prayer."

The younger children take it in at face value. Let God know what's going on, ask Him what you want, enjoy each other, and that's enough.

The older ones seem to think there must be something more important to prayer. With them I can get into world events: environmental, hunger, peace and justice issues. As they come into awareness of these issues through their classes or the media, we bring them up in prayer.

"But always," I tell them, "always include your own day and how things were for you—and make connections. For instance, when you study or read about environmental problems, you might want to ask yourself before God, what are you doing to help? How could you, in your circumstances, be involved? When you hear of the nuclear war threat (all have, sometimes a good number of children pray to be able to grow up), certainly pray about that. As you get older ask yourself before God what your responsibility as a Christian and as a citizen of a great country might be? Be realistic for your resources and your ability. Be realistic, too, about learning what you want to stand for. You need to test it out with God in your prayer."

"How do you do that?"

"Probably it will take longer than the time we give it in prayer room. When something concerns you, and you are struggling with what to do about it, bring it up with God in your heart. Get as quiet as you can and wait. You may know an answer. . . . It might take some days, or some weeks. Maybe you'll know what to do during your prayer time. Maybe the answer will come some other time during the day, or week."

A fifth grader's hand shot up into the air. "That's happened to me!" she said with some excitement. "I never told anyone, but sometimes I think God is telling me something when I am quiet with Him. The next day, or the day after that, other people tell me the same thing."

"Sure that happens," I said. "Often God uses other people to tell us things. The problem is: people tell us so many things. (They agreed.) We need to sort it out, and come to some sense of what is right. That's why we need quiet time with God."

In putting together the slides for this session, I had to think more than usual. From the kindergarten I had borrowed a box of large, colored wooden beads and a red and white string. I photographed them. First I had the string empty and the beads scattered on the table. Then the beads were progressively strung. That was the easy part. I needed these in among the other slides so that during the presentation there was a constant reminder to string the days events and people together, conscious of God's presence. With the upper grades there was the simple reminder of the metaphor being used. With the lower grades I'd ask, "What's your string?" and they'd answer, "day string, night string." We settled for "talking to God to hold the day together string!"

What to use for the larger number of slides? One thing I know is that children love animals. There seems to be a natural inclination to go out to all living things. So I filled the carousel with animals and birds. It would be attractive, I knew. To make the connection, we talked a bit about how each animal is itself naturally. If it isn't someone's pet or farm animal, it has to work hard to find food and keep alive. That's fine for animals. We have been given more by God, so we have more to enjoy and more decisions to make. We are able to know God better so we pray.

Upper grades looked at the slides with enjoyment. The lower grades did too. The very little ones called out the names of the animals as their images were projected. When there was an animal with which they were not familiar, (I had photographed them in a safari), there would be a pause, one little voice would guess, others would repeat the guess. At the end I'd ask the animal they liked best. The youngest almost always picked a domestic animal: a dog, a kitten, a cow. Middle grade children named farm animals or pets: especially goats, ducks, and deer . . . "because they are gentle. . . ." As the grades went up, the choices became more adventurous: "the lion . . . the tiger . . . they are always strong . . . brave . . . king of the forest."

The room was darkened for the slides. Changing the music to the tape of the Gregorian chant, I asked the children to get as comfortable as they wanted, staying alert and in their own space. Then, welcoming God in their hearts, give Him a tour of what was there. After that I suggested they spend a little time with God about stringing the day together with Him, going over their lives on a day to day basis and how they might do it together.

Then I encouraged them to think of all the people who love them and whom they love, and put them into their heart. God and they love those people together. Finally, they are with God alone. "Remember," I said to them again, "God always is present, and God always is loving us. Take these few moments and enjoy God's loving you, for He truly does."

At the end of the prayer, but while they were still quiet, I reminded them to give God a tour of their hearts—or to string beads in His presence—every night. Then take a little while to enjoy His loving them. We concluded, as usual, with the Lord's Prayer.

I thanked the children for coming and told them how much I enjoyed their company. They said they enjoyed mine and the animals, too!

In Summary

At the Day's End

1. Go over it with God: people, places, whatever happened.
2. Let God know how it was for you.
3. Let God see what pleased you, puzzled you, hurt you, made you afraid or ashamed or amused.
4. Quietly let *one thing* of the day come to you.
5. Spend some time with God about that one thing.
6. Rest quietly with Him, ready to hear Him or just enjoy being together.

For the Older Children

In addition, be aware of the issues of the day: locally, nationally, internationally, spend time with God:

1. about the issue and how it affects you
2. pondering what your responsibility might be
3. asking for whatever you need to carry out your responsibility

Be Aware

The more empty we become,
the more able we are
to hear God
and be filled
with Him.

Chapter 7

Calling Names

(Yours, Jesus', and What Isaiah Had to Say About Them)

It was getting closer to Christmas. There were two things I wanted to do with the children this time. One was to think about Christmas in terms of Jesus and of themselves. The other was to find out, after three months of meeting in the prayer room, what it was that the children liked best. That they liked the prayer room was obvious; they keep asking teachers and me when they can come back. What was it that we were doing right?

They came in, class after class, as if they had ingested Mexican jumping beans at all meals the day before. "Christmas spirit!" said the teachers, rolling their eyes upward. It took longer than usual for each child to have one pillow and find individual space.

One part of the brain kept reminding me, "They are guests." The other part of my brain kept saying, "They are children, and children just before Christmas. They are children, and children just before Christmas. Guest . . . children . . . Christmas time."

"We are going to start a bit differently today," I announced. "What I want you to do first is something you will need to be able to do if you intend to be any good at athletics, concentrating, or prayer. You have the same body whether you're using it for sports, study, or prayer." At least that caught their attention. "Sit erect, please. This works best if your spine is straight. Place your hands on your lap, palms upward. Now breathe in through your nose as I count to five. I am going to count slowly, so breathe quietly and slowly. One, two, three, four, five." (While counting I watch a clock: one second a number.) "Out, two, three, four, five. Hold for five; out for five. You will not all be able to do it. If you can't, that is all right. Do what you can and begin again. Ready. . . .

69

"*In,* two, three, four, five; *hold,* two, three, four, five; *out* two, three, four, five. Again. *In,* two, three, four, five; *hold,* two, three, four, five; *out,* two, three, four, five."

I watched their respiration carefully, especially the younger ones. The slow breathing was repeated several times. I encouraged them to do well, start over when they needed to, and to take their time. I was very aware it is difficult to breathe slowly, especially when they are full of jumping beans.

When they seemed to be calmer, I began to instruct, "Breathe at your own pace now. Relax and get comfortable. Close your eyes and breathe gently. Imagine yourself, here, in the prayer room all alone. The trees are here, the plants and the pillows, but you are the *only person.* There is a big pile of plastic bags in the room. They are meant for your use. What you are doing, in your imagination, is thinking of all things you like about the prayer room. You are also remembering all the things that we did in the prayer room together. As you remember each, put it into the plastic bag. Tie it and put it into the middle of the room.

"First think of what you saw when you came into the prayer room: the trees, and the plants. Put them into a bag and tie it. Place it in the middle of the room. You saw the stained glass unicorn and then the chunky glass crucifix. Put them into a plastic bag. Tie it and put it in the center of the room."

The younger children gestured picking the bags up and putting them down. A boy or two had fun throwing them. Imaginatively, of course.

"We talked about prayer being like a milkstool. We looked at dandelions and saw how much prettier they are up close—like people whom we know and love. We strung beads . . . and looked at animals. Put all of those images into a bag. Tie it and put it in the middle of the room.

"In our imagination we saw God and ourselves as a tree and once we saw ourselves and others as toys. Put the phantasies into another bag. Tie it and place it into the middle of the room. It might be getting a bit crowded, but there is plenty of space.

"Everytime you came into the prayer room, we had music. Put the music in a bag and do the same as before. Then we always got quiet and invite God into our hearts. Put the quiet time into a bag. Tie it and put it into the middle of the room.

"Now, what personally do you like about the prayer room besides all of these things? You have in your imagination all the bags you need so take all you want."

I waited a few minutes, watching the gestures of the little ones, and the rapid eye movements of the older children. When they seemed about ready, the next instruction followed.

"Walk around all the bags you have piled up. Walk around them slowly a few times. Remember, anything is possible in imagination. Something a little peculiar is about to happen. As you are walking around the bags, one will sort of come towards your hand. Just one will. Reach out and take that one out of your pile. Go to the side of the room, and open your bag. Look at what is in that one bag."*

Because it is important for each one to hear his/her own voice saying what happened in the phantasy, I invited the children, in groups of four, to say what they found in their respective bags. This also served the purpose in the junior high grades, for the youngsters to share the kinds of things that were found without necessarily saying their own publicly. ("Tell me what sorts of things were said in your group?")

In giving suggestions about what they may like, how could I have overlooked the large pillows? In every class some always liked that—if not the best, at least as part of, the best.

In each class I took a few responses to what they liked best.

Seventh grade Jen: "I like it best that the whole class prays together."

Seventh grade Jack: "I like the silent prayer a lot."

Eighth grade Frank: "I like the use of cushions during discussion. And being quiet and relaxed."

Kindergarteners reported liking movies, dreams, and music; but best of all, "asking God to come to my heart and He comes."

Second grade Elizabeth: "God loving me."

Fourth grade Lenny: "In my bag I had music and candy." Then he added, "You should pick up leaves around the tree." (Weeping fig trees weep!)

*This phantasy is adapted from a similar one in *Imagine That!*, Marlene Halpin (Dubuque: Wm. C. Brown Company Publishers, 1981). It is a good phantasy to use whenever there are many things to deal with and you want to isolate one thing at a time for a person.

Fourth grade Lenny: "In my bag I had music and candy." Then he added, "You should pick up leaves around the tree." (Weeping fig trees weep!)

Third grade Billy: "Dreams about God."

Eighth grade Ellen: "I think it is fun to think about things and God and I liked sitting on the pillow."

Eighth grade Carole: I like it when you talk about different ways to pray—blessing and thanking God. I never would have thought about them."

First grade Patty: "I love it when God comes in my heart."

Eighth grade Chrissy: "I like all the kids together, doing the same thing with God."

Third grade Julie: "Dandelions."

Second grade Norrie: "I saw a pumping heart with the word "love" coming out."

Seventh grade Pete: "I like inviting God to be with me, and stringing my day."

Time had to be watched, and I wanted to move into a Christmas theme. Therefore I asked the teachers if they would be willing to do a follow up for me, and ask the children in their classrooms. "I'd like it too," I told the teachers, "if you would add your own favorite thing from the prayer room." The teachers did. Some of them asked the children orally and sent me a summary; some had the classes write it out. A sampling of responses runs like this:

Fifth grade Cindy: "A string of beads were in my bag. I like the slides and the music that went with it."

Sixth grade Harry: "Prayer together, toys, beads, film. The big thing that I liked best was the deep, deep thinking with God."

Fourth grade Don: "In my bag I had candy, girls, dogs, cats, birds, flowers, trees, love, ice cream, food, money, water and fish."

First grade Roy: "Music with God."

Third grade Lee: "I found the private prayers. I like it the best."

Second grade Ann: "I like the movies and I like you. Best of all I like to imagine things."

Fifth grade Ken: "Most of all I like the dandelions and the beads."

Fifth grade Reggie: I like it best when we sit on the cushions and lay relaxed and talk about God on the cushion."

Fourth grade Cheryl: "My silent prayer and the God tree."

Kindergarten Mark: "My bag had God and my dog."

"I like the atmosphere where I can feel God's presence in me and others."

"I like the peace of it."

"Truly it is a quiet time. You accept the students as they are emotionally: high, low, frisky, pensive, etc."

"You are aware of their needs without embarrassing them or invading their privacy."

"I like the way you make all of us feel good about ourselves and self-worth coming from that."

"I like having the time almost to myself, and I can pray, too."

When I went through the materials the teachers returned to me, I found heading the list a combination of peace and quiet; God in my heart; relaxing; different ways to think about God, and the slides—sharing first place for favorites. Music and doing imaginative things were the next most popular. No one session stood out more than the others; nor was any session left out of the list completely. I was pleased with the results of the bag phantasy.

In the prayer room during the last meeting before Christmas, I used the theme of names.

"I'm going to ask you to do something I suppose you've never done before in school. When I count to three, I want everyone in the room to say your own name out loud. One, two, three."

They did, but so softly I could hardly even hear it even though there were twenty or more voices speaking together.

"Oh, you can do better than that! Your name is so important—it means *you*. When I count to three say your name loud enough for the person next to you to hear, if that person weren't so busy talking loud, too. One, two, three." Names came much louder. (Children, guests, jumping beans.) "Good! Is there anyone in the classroom who has a little brother or sister?" Always there are some. "Do you remember before your little brother or sister was born?" Always there are some. "What did you talk about concerning the baby before he or she came?"

"My dad said he didn't care whether it was a boy or a girl; he just wanted a strong, healthy baby . . . but I wanted a brother."

"Did you and your father both get your wishes?"

"Yup," with a big smile.

"What else did some of you talk about?"

"We kept wondering what to call the baby if it was a boy or girl."

"Why do you think that might be important?"

"Well, it's its name!" The emphasis on *name* explained it all.

"Yes, it is; it is very important. You just got to say your names out loud. How many of you were named after someone?" Usually more than half of the class raises their hands.

"After whom were you named?" The responses included parents, grandparents, aunts and uncles, special friends, someone admired, a special saint.

"If you were named for someone, what might you see in the way your name was selected?" The question was beyond the youngest: from the middle grades up they came to, "It was someone my mom and dad loved."

"Yes, and what might that tell you?"

"They love me, too." Oh, the smiles and bright eyes that came with that statement!

"What about people like me?" asked Jeremiah, "No one in my family has my name. But my father keeps telling me it's a strong name, and my mother said it always was her favorite name for a man."

"You tell me what that means."

Jeremiah thought. "Well, they both liked it."

"And?"

"I guess they wanted me to have something they both liked, because they like me!" A slow smile came with his insight.

"I guess so! How many others have names their parents really like?" A scattering of hands went up. "Do you suppose the same thing is true of you? Do you suppose your parents cared enough about you to give you a name they especially liked?" They thought so, and looked pleased.

"One more question about your names. How many of you have nicknames?" Most of the hands went up. "Okay, let's do the same thing as we did with your name. When I count to three everyone say your nickname aloud."

"What if you have more than one?" a worried Sarah, with frown lines between her eyes asked.

"Then talk fast and say them all."

"One, two, three!" This time I didn't have to tell them to say their names loud!

"How many of you are willing to say your special names to the class?"

Most were derivatives of longer names. Some were Butch . . . Sunshine . . . Pearl . . . Pet . . . Love . . . Precious . . . My girl . . . Princess . . . My Little Man . . . Dear . . . Honey. . . .

Again, to watch the faces of the children as they just about whispered these endearments was a reverent thing. Those who spoke were obviously loved children, being aware of their being loved.

"There is one most special name which we are going to think about today. The Bible calls this 'the name above all names.' Why do you think this might be?" There was some guessing. "God, the saints, the Blessed Mother, Jesus!" It never took long to get the name of Jesus.

"Yes, and why do you think that the name of Jesus is so super-special?

Sooner or later they came to His being God, His loving us, His coming to save us, God's coming to be with us, His teaching us what is right and what we should do to go to heaven.

"Everything you say is right," I told them. "And remember, Jesus told us that whatever we ask the Father in His name, we shall receive. We'll talk about that some more another day, but for now remember: the name of Jesus is the most powerful name in the whole world. It's a very special name we all want to keep in our minds and hearts, and love very much. In a few moments we shall look at pictures of Jesus' birthday. When is Jesus' birthday? Christmas, of course!"

"The slides we are going to look at are photographs of great paintings. Now, in a way, they can't all be exactly true because they are painted in different countries and in different centuries. Since Jesus came for all people, people paint Jesus, Mary, Joseph, the angels, and the shepherds like they are. (This school is racially very mixed with Orientals, Caucasions, Blacks, Hispanics—literally the children's parents come from all over the earth. Many are not Catholic although most are Christian. When there is a class with a Moslem or Hindu child, I suggest to the child to think of his or her own holy book. Do they know it, and the name for

God in their tradition? They do. Then I tell them to use their holy book in their mind and heart.) You will see a variety of ways of showing Bethlehem. What is the same, though, is that God sent His son to love and to teach us and show us how to be happy. That is what is important.

"The music this time will be different. There is a singer on the tape. He is a priest whose name is Carey Landry. He's singing a song called, "By Name I Have Called You." Father Landry rewrote the words a little to fit the music, but the basic words he uses are very ancient ones taken from the Hebrew Scriptures. There was a prophet by the name of Isaiah, and in his book in the Bible you can find words like these,

"Do not be afraid. I have called you by name. . . ."

"God called me before I was born, from my mother's womb He said my name. . . ."

"No matter who forgets you, God will never forget you. . . ."

(Isaiah 43:1; 45:3; 49:1)

"You will hear words like these on the tape while we look at the slides."

As I drew the shades, one of the children put the lights out and all of them settled in to look at the blank white wall. For this slide session I used slides of the great nativity masterpieces. In between, because we were talking about names and how precious each of us is in God's sight, I used pictures of the children I had taken over the last few months. They were delighted and excited. One of my pleasures in watching them was their pleasure not only when it was their own image, but when a brother or a sister, a friend or someone who rides the bus, appeared. When the principal, pastors, teachers or secretaries also appeared, they laughed and clapped. "Well," I laughed with them, "we all are called by name, and all are precious to God."

Unlike other times, I used the same tape for prayer. Lights remained out; shades remained drawn and the slide projector was turned off. "Make yourselves as comfortable as you like," I invited them. "Welcome God into your heart and give Him a tour of what is going on in your life. Tell Him—any way you want. Whether you use words or feelings or just know each other—tell Him how you feel about His calling you by name since before you were born. Let Him know from you how you feel about His being so concerned about you, loving you so much that He called you by name even before you were born. . . ."

Now put into your heart all the people you love and who love you. . . . This time, pay special attention to your mother and father and your grandparents who gave you life and named you . . . you and God look at them together. Love them together . . . if there is anything special about any of them, let God know it from you . . . and love them together, again.

"Now let them fade away and pay attention just to God and to yourself. You know God is always with you and always loves you. This time I want you to listen to the words of the Bible and to Father Landry singing them. Everytime he sings about calling you by name, you say your own name and hear God telling you how precious you are to Him and how He loves you because you are His."

I turned on the cassette player, and when those lines came, (they are repeated several times), I said gently, "Say your name . . . God is talking to you."

When the tape was over, I left the children alone for a moment. It was too intimate a time to interrupt. "Keep very aware of God in your heart and His great love for you. Open your eyes gently and sit up slowly." When they had, "Let's end this session by praying together the prayer that Jesus, who has the greatest name of all, taught us to pray, Our Father. . . ." Class after class the children barely whispered through it. They left the room much more quietly than they had come in, and with some wonder and joy showing.

Later that day I met Mary Ann, the principal. She looked at me and laughed. "I met little Joyce in the hall before," she said, and told her I saw her picture among the Christmas slides.

"Oh yes," Joyce responded seriously, "I was there when Sister took my picture."

In Summary

Breathing

When children are unusually active, their high energy is ready to channeled. (Fighting children's energy is a waste of our energy and time!)

Breathing is a natural and good way to help them turn energy inward productively.

1. Attend only to breathing. When other thoughts come (and they will) acknowledge them, let them go, and pay attention to your breathing.
2. Count
   • Count for inhale and exhale, pacing them evenly perhaps to a count of five (or whatever suits the age group and energy level—sometimes start with a count of three and increase as seems appropriate).
   • If more stillness is wanted, and if the children are able, count for inhale, pause, exhale, pacing them evenly.
   • For older children, the pause breathing might be extended to count for inhale, pause, exhale, pause, pacing them evenly. (Try this yourself until you are comfortable with it before doing it with a class.)

N. B. At all times, watch respiration and allow for individual differences.

Praying

Children evidence delight in knowing that:

1. They are praying.
2. Others are praying, too
   at the same time, and
   in the same place.

There is strength and comfort in each other's praying presence.

Names

1. Use Scripture to reinforce their own natural love for their names—meaning their own person.
2. Use prayerful being with God to:
   - hear His calling each by name.
   - Thank Him for parents and grandparents who gave life and name.

Be Aware

Of the great love:

God's and your parents'
which brought forth your life,
and your being called
by name.

Chapter 8

Take Me!

(My Picture—Jesus and the Woman at the Well)

I was in the school playground during lunch hour hoping (foolishly) to photograph some of the children at play. Somewhere or other I had read that someone human needs to be shown among non-human slides, at least every 7 or 8 of them. Since I use so many nature slides symbolically, the humans I seed among them are generally the children themselves. It always pleases them. Occasionally they borrow the slide to bring home. At any rate, I hoped to photograph some of them playing. The minute they saw the camera I was deluged with, "Sister, take me! . . . Take me!"

Becky, a second grader, came up softly and didn't say, "Take me!" Her request was, "Sister, make me a prayer." Terry was on one side of her and Dennis on the other. "Well, Becky," I said to her, "what do you want to ask of God?"

Her lovely green eyes slid off into the middle distance. I watched the sun glint on her long hair. "I want . . ." she began hesitantly, "I want . . ." Then she picked up speed: "I want God to love me very much!"

"He does that already!" Dennis yelled with a disgusted look on his face. "That's dumb! Why don't you ask for something you *don't* have?" Terry agreed.

Becky smiled her front-tooth-missing smile. "All right. I want . . . I want the sun to shine and . . . and . . . the birds to sing some more . . . and . . . and . . . to have a good time this summer!"

"Me, too!" said Terry fervently.

"How do you think we could make this a prayer," I asked them.

"We could say the Our Father." This came from Dennis.

Becky started and the others joined in: "Our Father, who art in heaven. . . ."

When it was completed two pairs of brown and one pair of green eyes looked at me and waited.

"That was fine," I told them.

Smiles.

"Now what else do you think we could do to make the prayer Becky asked for?" Two pairs of brown and one pair of green eyes looked at me, waiting, again.

I began, "Dear God,"

"Dear God," they repeated.

". . . You heard what Becky said, and You know what is in Terry's and Dennis' (two big grins, also with front teeth missing) hearts, too. Please let it all come true, as long as it makes all of us happy. We trust you to know what makes us happy, and we love you, and thank you for loving us."

The three children, standing on the edge of the playground in the noon day sun, repeated the simple prayer, phrase by phrase. Silence.

It was Dennis again who spoke first, this time with excitement. "I can do that at home! I can do that at night!"

"Sure you can. Whatever you want to tell God, tell Him, and tell Him you trust Him to answer all your prayers in a way that will make you happy."

Becky is a hugger. She hugged me, and the three of them ran off to play.

In the meantime the other children had gone back to their games. I tried again to photograph them, with a little success. They came running and calling, "Take me! Take me!" Heads up, necks stretched, grins, two fingers spread behind other children's heads. How could I convince them that a telephoto lens—so good for photographing just faces—doesn't allow groups to fit in. Let them look through the viewfinder and see what I see? A few could; there were too many present for that to be effective. Let them think that all are being photographed when in effect, only two or three are? There would be too much disappointment when the slides came back and they were missing. So, I told them, "Get yourselves together with your friends. When I have taken your part of the group,

I'll let you know." Some of them, enough of them, heard me to make it effective.

Finally, "That's it for today. All my film is used up."

Groans. "When will you get more?"

"When I get more money."

Children understand that. They went back to the monkey bars and swings, the jump ropes and marbles. And I went back to the prayer room to meet my next class.

John's Gospel, "the Woman at the Well with Jesus" story: I never tire of it. Most of my friends don't either. Maybe that would be a good section for the children, I thought.

"Does anyone know what a well is?" I asked the first grade.

"It's where you get water."

"You need a bucket."

"That's where the frogs are—everybody knows *that!*"

"What's the one, most important thing?"

"Water!" they chorused.

"Right. We all need water to live. Here, in our part of the country, we are blessed with a good water supply. What do you use water for?"

"To drink . . . to wash . . . to wash your clothes . . . to water the lawn . . . to put in my gerbils' cage . . . to do laundry . . . for water fights . . . to swim in . . . to ride a boat on . . . to go fishing in. . . ."

"All of you are right. We can't live without water. Water is very important to the story we are going to talk about, and pray from today.

Jesus and his friends had a long way to walk. The part of the country they were walking through was very sandy and dry, and didn't have many trees. Finally they came to a place where there was a town, a town where the people weren't very friendly to them.

Those other people believed in God, too, but they worshipped Him differently from the Jews. Sometimes when people worship differently they think they are so right that they do not treat other people with respect. Did any of you ever have that kind of experience?"

The little ones, if they did, weren't aware of it. The bigger children, some of them, nodded thoughtfully. I didn't want to pursue it, beyond making a point. So I went on:

"I think everybody deserves respect. We don't have to agree, nor do we have to have the same convictions, but we do have to treat each other well." They agreed, in theory, anyway.

"Jesus was tired, the Bible tells us. His friends were considerate. They suggested he sit by the well outside of the town. That way Jesus could rest while they went into the town to buy some food for a meal. Wasn't that thoughtful of them to take care of Jesus like that? And Jesus must have really been tired; He let them take care of Him. Might that tell us something about how we should treat each other?"

The little ones told how their parents take care of them. The older ones were a bit more thoughtful when I asked how they might help take care of their parents—as the apostles did Jesus.

"Jesus was just sitting there when a woman came out with a bucket. Does anyone see anything surprising about that?" No one did. "Would you see anything exceptional in it if I added it was noon time?" They didn't—except for Jake who said, "Well, it was lunch time, and maybe she needed water to make lemonade".

"Maybe she did," I went on. "What was peculiar is that she came at noon. You see, when we want water, all we do is go to the sink and turn the faucet on. People in those days had to go where the well was, and lower a bucket."

"They could go to a stream—that would make it easier. We do that in the country sometimes," responded practical Dolores. "But even then," many added, "you have to be sure that the water isn't po—po—polluted!"

"That is true. Where Jesus was at this time there were no streams. You see, it was a dry land, and water was very, very precious. The weather was very, very hot. You know how hot it can get in the summer. It was like that. When it is summer, and when we have very hot days, what is the coolest part of the day?"

"When the air conditioner is on," readily came from Billy.

"Right! What about outside?" Eventually we got to early morning and evening.

"That is so. People in Jesus time, came to the well early in the morning and in the evening. Water is heavy to carry, and it is a hot walk. This lady came out at noon. Now can you guess why that was surprising?"

"Maybe she ran out of water," mused Gerry.

"Maybe the neighbors didn't have any extra to lend her," suggested Missy.

"She could get more if no one else was in line," from eighth grade Bart.

"There wouldn't be any pushing and shoving if she was alone," fifth grade Bob added.

"I'd go at noon. I don't like to wait." Tessie said.

"You all have a point," I added: "There's one more thing. She didn't want to meet anybody. She decided that if she went at noon, no one else would be there and that way she could avoid the neighbors. Now why do you suppose she might want to avoid the neighbors?"

"Because they didn't like her!" Upper grades generally came close to a chorus on that. Five and six year olds, as a class, seemed to have little experience of people not liking them. The older ones certainly did!

"You're right. They didn't like her. In their opinion this lady was living in a way that they disagreed with. Now it's OK to disagree with another person's behavior—sometimes that may be important for us to do. But we need to treat the person well. In this case the woman evidently had had experience of other people being mean to her. Have you ever been treated meanly?" Most of them said they had.

"When you are treated meanly, what did you want to do?"

Well, they had wanted to do many things, from harming the other person in a variety of ways, increasingly imaginative and gruesome as the ages went up, to withdrawing and not wanting to see them again. Sometimes, not wanting to see anyone.

"Now let's look at what happened with Jesus and the woman. It's important to do that because we can learn from Jesus how we can treat people best. The good part is that when we treat other people well we are also showing respect for ourselves. We don't want to be mean people, do we? Of course not!

"Imagine this. Jesus, all tired out, is sitting by the well on a hot day. He's waiting for his friends to come back. Unexpectedly a woman comes out for water. Remember, in Jesus time and in his culture, men and women weren't sociable in public places.

"Besides, this woman was a Samaritan—and Samaritans and Jews (Jesus was a Jew, right?) didn't mix socially. There they were.

No place for them to go. If you were in the woman's place, how do you think you would have felt?"

Junior high girls were quite sympathetic; the boys listened as the girls said things like:

"I'd be embarrassed."

"I'd probably leave without getting the water."

"I guess I'd be fresh even though I really wouldn't feel that way."

"I think that's what the woman did—got a bit sarcastic in the beginning of the conversation. Look at how it's related in the fourth chapter of St. John's gospel."

For the younger children, I just told the story. With the older children I went through the gospel account from the Bible. What I generally find very effective is to have a male and a female voice reading the dialogue with the explanatory phrases omitted. One interpretation of the scene allows the woman to begin with sarcastic: "What! *You, a Jew,* ask *me* a Samaritan for a drink!" Then watch the progression, as Jesus and she continued the conversation as the dialogue went on from her calling him a "Jew," to "Sir," to "prophet," to "Messiah." That is some progress in the course of a short conversation!

The children were suitably impressed. "She might well have been embarrassed and wanted to go away; she probably did start out ready for a fight. Why do you think it turned out so well?"

"Because of the way Jesus treated her." That answer came, in different words, from just about every grade.

"Right on target! How did Jesus treat her?"

"Fair. . . kind . . . sweet . . . love . . . with care," came from the younger ones.

"Like any other person!" bellowed a fourth grade black girl.

"With respect!" came from a chunky hispanic sixth grader.

"He really had a discussion with her," seventh grade Les observed.

"They talked a lot to each other," was third grade Alice's remark.

"Before we look at the slides, we have even more to think about. Let's go back to Jesus' words. He talks about "living water." I wonder a lot why Jesus makes water so important. We already talked about how important it is for physical life. I think Jesus was saying water, as a symbol, is important for the life of our spirit. Let's think about water for another few minutes. What's water composed of?"

"H_2O."

"Yes—water always is H_2O. Water responds to all the known temperatures on earth: generally we use it as a liquid. What happens when it is very cold? It freezes. Then we have snow or ice or hail. It still is H_2O. Water takes the shape of whatever we pour it into. Water might reflect the color of whatever it is near. Whatever shape of color it takes, always it is H_2O. What do you think that might mean for us?"

After some discussion we generally came to the idea of integrity. Most children are very, very aware of fairness. "That's not fair!" is a hot and spontaneous objection to some treatment. It's not difficult to move from a notion of fairness to one of integrity: of being fair inside of ourselves. How important it is, I suggest to them, that what we think and how we act and what we say and do fit together. It's not fair to ourselves, and it's not fair to the God who made us good, for us to think one way and act another, or to lie. It's just not fair. We can be with all kinds of people, in all sorts of situation, and what we really need to do is be ourselves and act the way Jesus taught us to act. Just like water is always H_2O no matter if it is hot and steamy, ordinary and liquid, cold and icy— it is H_2O. No matter if we are with friends, or people who treat us meanly, or people who even ignore us: we are fair with ourselves only if we stay ourselves and don't put on an act and behave other than we are, by being mean and nasty in return; or behave in a way pretending we are better than we are. Notice, I said, *pretending*. That doesn't mean trying to be better and practicing it. It means that we pretend and have no intention of learning to behave better. That's false and unfair. It's called hypocrisy.

The fourth grade teacher told me some of the youngsters were threatening each other. Could that come up in the prayer room? It could.

"Sometimes children, sometimes adults, threaten each other." There was silence . . . very silent silence. "In this gospel story, Jesus had everything on His side to threaten the woman: He was a man, He was a Jew, and He was at the well first. Did He threaten her?"

"No."

"Why do you think He didn't?"

"It doesn't go anywhere," came thoughtfully from a child in a boy scout uniform. I could have hugged him. Instead I repeated his statement.

"It doesn't go anywhere—that is, anywhere that will make us or the other person happy and proud of ourselves. The one who threatens often can't do what he or she is threatening: so it's a mean thing to do, and sometimes it's a lie. Sometimes it is cruel because it makes the other person worry a lot. Sometimes it gets both people into trouble. It's something Jesus didn't do with the woman, did He? If you think about it, He didn't threaten her, but He did tell her the truth. It was not pleasant. She had done things which were not the best things to do. Jesus faced her with the truth. He did not threaten her. That left her free to look at what she had done and make up her mind to act differently. Most people are like that. Most of us don't really change our behavior for long because of threats. We just adjust as long as we feel we have to and then go back to the same way of acting. Jesus way is so much better. He didn't make the woman worry about threats, and He doesn't make us worry about threats. He asks us to look at our behavior and its consequences. Pointing out consequences of our behavior is part of telling the truth, and part of respect. People don't always think about what it will be like, living out the consequences of what we do. Jesus didn't threaten; He did tell the truth and the woman responded well. We can all learn from that."

"One more thought. The slides we are going to see won't make much sense if we don't have this idea. Jesus tells us He is willing to give us "living water," life for our spirit. He says that the water He will give us will be like a spring, or a fountain, welling up within us—so that we will be able to live really happy lives. The thing of it is, we need to ask God's help and God's blessing. Also, we need to be willing to receive His help no matter how he sends it. For the sake of the example today, we'll look at images of water— water coming as big as an ocean or as small as a drop on the rim of a leaky faucet. What I'd suggest you think about is how water always is H_2O, and how we need to ask for the living water and to receive it no matter how God sends it.

"Ready?" They were.

One of the children put the lights out while I drew the shades and started Galways' *Songs of the Seashore* played with the Tokyo orchestra. It is lovely and lively music. To begin the slides sequence I used photographs of the statues at Notre Dame University: Jesus sitting on the edge of a well, the woman across the well from him. It is a lovely, larger than life size grouping. Instead of seeing the slides of water with living people, I seeded the water slides with different angles of Jesus and the woman.

When the slides had been viewed, I kept the room dimmed as usual and invited the children to get as comfortable as they pleased, but to stay alert. They wiggled into more comfort and closed their eyes.

"Welcome God into your heart. Tell Him, or show Him, or let Him know—however you choose—how you are, and what is going on in your life. Let Him know, from you personally, what you think about that story of Jesus and the woman at the well, and how they treated each other."

Tell Him, or show Him, or let Him know how you tend to treat people—especially someone you might think isn't as good as you are. . . . Tell Him, or show Him, or let Him know from you, what it's like for you when someone treats you unfairly. . . . Now be quiet a moment in case God wants you to learn something from the way Jesus and that woman talked with each other."

After a few quiet minutes (I never, never ask the children to share this part of the session together. I judge it to be too intimate, too precious and too private for them to articulate in front of other children. Often enough they come and talk privately about it—or with a best friend.) I encourage them to put into their heart all the people who love them, and whom they love. Looking at them with God, let Him know from you whatever special or different is going on; then the two of you love all those people together. . . . Again, after a few moments: "You and God be alone together now. Remember always He is present, always He is loving us. What we need to do is remember, and enjoy His loving us. Take these few minutes to enjoy God's loving you."

We ended as usual opening eyes slowly, sitting up gently, being by ourselves a moment and then praying the prayer Jesus taught us to pray.

I thanked the children for coming, telling them how much I enjoyed their company. That is the truth—I do. On the way out of the room a first grader hugged me somewhere around the middle, saying, "I love the whole, whole world."

A second grader beckoned me down to his mouth level and whispered, "We are adopting a baby, but we can't tell anyone yet."

"Are you happy about that?" I asked him.

"Yes," he whispered back, "I don't even care if it is a boy or a girl. We are going to love the baby very much."

"Good! I am sure you will. Will you let me know when the baby comes?"

"Yes," He scampered off to rejoin his class.

In Summary

Using Scripture

When using a scripture story, saturate the children and yourself in it:

1. Review the salient elements ("What's a well?" City children need to be asked).
2. Repeat the use of the elements in the story.
3. As appropriate, discuss the symbolism of the elements.
4. Talk about the meaning of the story:
   - in scripture
   - for us

Prayer

Follow with the usual quiet prayer time, allowing reflection/praying time for each child to:

- integrate meanings of the story into his/her own life, and
- respond to God personally.

Be Aware

Bible Stories

are everlastingly rich
for each of us,

Allowing new insights

as our living
is ever new.

Chapter 9

Nothing In Between

(The Potter's Hands and the Clay)*

On my desk early that winter morning was a crayoned card. Under a big smiling face, it read: "You are my favorite God Lady". Jessica, a third grader, came in later to see how I liked it. I liked it very much, and told her so. "God Lady" to Jessica, "Prayer Sister" to most of the rest of the school. The prayer room was featured in the junior high paper under an article headed, "PR for God"—PR indeed. The children are certainly products of the age, I thought. I wonder how they are going to take to Jeremiah.

I wanted to introduce them to Jeremiah the prophet . . . Jeremiah who suffered so much he just about thought he could suffer no more . . . Jeremiah who did what God wanted and was often in trouble over it with his countrymen . . . Jeremiah who had decided he had had enough, and would not preach God's message anymore . . . And Jeremiah who found out that the fire in his heart, the fire in his bones, took more effort to restrain than preaching about God did . . . Jeremiah whose life was a living relationship to his God. I wondered how the children were going to take Jeremiah. But first, I would start with questions.

This time when I greeted the children a Rampal tape was playing. That flute is beautiful and calming. They came in, took a pillow, and were becoming accustomed to finding their own space. One or another still tested (two pillows), but by and large they spread out around the room. Being in the coatroom recess was still the prized place. Fitting a pillow between the larger tree and the tall, standing plants was the next best. What energy the chil-

*See Jeremiah 18:1–7.

dren use to *walk* across the room, when they want to be first in the special space!

After all were settled down, I asked if they had been praying like this at home. More than half, over all the school, said that they did. One or another complained that it was hard to get started. Several children said that they found it hard to pray with their eyes closed.

"Oh, I'm glad you are bringing those things up," I told them. Let's start with the second thing first. If you find it hard to pray with your eyes closed, then pray with them open. There is nothing particularly important about that. What is important is that you find a way which allows you to concentrate, which cuts off the ordinary things which interest you and would take your attention away from God. For instance, if your eyes are open and you are praying near a TV set, it might be harder to keep on praying. If your eyes are closed, you might not think so much about turning it on. For those of you who have difficulty in praying with your eyes closed, by all means, keep them open. What might be useful is to look at something neutral. For instance, you might look at your foot or at your hands in your lap. Do whatever serves being quiet and with God. Does that help?" It seemed to. "I like looking at the sun coming through the crucifix when I pray," said Judy "Is that OK?" Before I could answer Mark added, "I like looking at the plants, especially that one hanging to the floor." "Good! Keep right on.

"As for the problem of getting started by yourself, I suppose I didn't make it clear enough for you. Here, in the prayer room in school, we meet in classes. That means, of course, that there are twenty or more children and two adults—your teacher and me. We need a little time to settle in together and to prepare to pray together. At home you are probably by yourself, aren't you?" Most of them were. "Then there is the question of something for all of us to talk about. Because I'm the teacher, part of my responsibility is to prepare it for you. You don't need to do that. There is music when you come into the room, during the slides and during the prayer. I select that carefully for you. That is part of my job, too. You don't need to do that.

"Suppose you like music?" Ruthie questioned.

"What are you asking me?" I replied.

"Well," Ruthie said, "I like to play music in my room."

"So do I," I told her. "The question here is: does the music help you get quiet so you can welcome God into your heart and spend time with Him alone; or does the music get inside you so that you pay attention to the music, and not to God in your heart?"

Ruthie thought a moment and then said, "It depends on the music I play."

"That's a good answer—and you really have answered yourself, haven't you? If you pick music that will get you singing and listening intently to it, then that might not be the best music to play for prayer time. If you play music which helps if you get quiet and concentrate on God and your life, then that is good music for prayer. The same thing applies here: Do what helps you to be aware of God's presence and God's loving you."

"OK," said Ruthie, "I see what you mean. I can do that."

"Fine. . . . Here we use slides, too. Again, I do that for you as a teacher."

"What if we have a special picture at home that we like to look at?"

Al added to that, "I have one. I always feel real good when I look at it for a long time." "Same answer as with music," I said. "If looking at the picture helps you to get quiet inside with God in your heart, use it for prayer. If the picture absorbs you so that all your attention is on the picture, or how it was done, or memories you have of the place and that takes over your consciousness, by all means go on enjoying it. But enjoy it outside of your quiet time with God. Does that make sense to you?" It did.

"I can't make up dreams by myself." That statement was from Jeannie in the fourth grade.

"You mean the phantasies, like the God tree?" She did.

"Oh, of course you can't! And it isn't important that you do. Thank you for saying that. That's just another way to get to know ourselves better, and to start some time being with God. There are many, many ways we can be with God. Just because you can't do one or another by yourself, don't let that stop you! Find the ways that you like best and use them. Please, don't worry about the phantasies. When we do them together, enjoy them and learn from them. At home, don't bother your head about them. OK?" OK.

"What you need to do at home," I continued, "is to find a place where you can be quiet. If you want to be with your parents or brothers or sisters, that's fine. If you want to be alone, that's fine. If you want it one way one time and a different way another time, that's fine, too." ("That's fine," murmured a few kindergarten children with little smiles.)

"The really important thing," I reminded them, "is to be aware that God *is* with you. Know that He is with you and loving you; let Him know from you what is going on in your life. Let Him know from you what is happening, how you feel about it, what you are going to do about it. When you are puzzled or uncertain, ask for guidance to make good decisions. When you are angry or sad, let Him know why—and ask for help. When you are happy or excited, tell Him, or show Him, and thank Him. You see, praying is living a relationship with God. That means you tell each other about each other. What you have to tell is what you are experiencing that day. Then you listen for awhile. It's all very simple, really."

"You mean," Walt said, "that the end part of what we do in the prayer room is what we do at home? Clue God in on the day, look at the people we love together, and then just have fun hanging around along with God. Is that what you mean?" "That's what I mean."

The children looked satisfied. There were no more questions that day, from them. I asked them: "*When* did Jesus pray?"

One five year old started; two others followed in quick succession:

"Jesus prayed on Christmas!"

"And on Easter!"

"And on the Fourth of July!"

"And Thanksgiving!" Julie settled back with a satisfied smile. "Do you mean that He prayed on special days?" Yes, that is what they meant, and that was a good meaning. When else?

Throughout the grades the children (and later, their parents) tried hard to remember gospel stories.

"Jesus prayed at parties . . . like when they needed wine at a wedding and His mom asked Him to do something about it."

"He prayed in the Garden because bad things were going to happen to Him, and He was scared."

"Yeah, and His friends zonked out on Him, so He was alone."

"He prayed at the Last Supper and gave us First Communion."

"He prayed on the cross and asked God to forgive the bad men."

"On the cross, He asked His best friend to take care of His mom."

"He prayed to make food for all the people who came to listen to Him."

"He sometimes prayed when people were dead, and He made them alive again."

"He prayed for us that we'd all go to heaven."

"Jesus liked little kids."

They did well, the children did. Few remembered Jesus' praying before He made important decisions—like when He spent forty days in the desert, then had those temptations, got baptized and chose His apostles. Nor did they generally remember Jesus' praying when He was happy—like when the apostles came back from their first time preaching and reported success. The children did well, remembering most of the stories. Their teachers looked proud of them.

"*Where* did Jesus pray?" was the second question I put to them.

"In church where His mom and dad found Him when they thought he was lost."

"At home."

"Wherever people were."

"Wherever people were who needed Him."

"Up on the mountain or out in the desert."

"In His heart . . . like we do?" Toby wasn't altogether sure, but he hoped so.

"*Who was around* when Jesus prayed?"

"His mom."

"The apostles."

"The people."

"Sometimes He was alone."

"All of you are correct. Every single answer is right. Now I want you to think. Think back over what you said about *when* Jesus prayed and *where* and *with whom*. If you put it altogether, what do you think about the way Jesus prayed?"

"He prayed all . . . the . . . time!" The surprise and delight on the young faces was a joy to behold. "He prayed anywhere, anytime." "He prayed about whatever came along." "It didn't matter who the people were—like His friend Lazarus, or the lady crying because her son died, or even that lady at the well—He prayed with everybody." They had gotten the point, and well.

"You are so right!" I said to them. "You are absolutely right. Now tell me something else. If we are supposed to be like Jesus, what do you think that this has to do with us?"

"I guess it means we should pray all over the place," blurted out Will. Then he looked surprised at himself.

"I guess it does," I agreed. "How do you think we might manage that? After all, we are busy people with lots of things to do."

"We can pray while stringing beads at night. I like to do that," remarked Liz. "Or you can do it in a hurry . . . you know, if you can show God in feelings, well, when you're feeling something, you can sort of just let God know right away."

"Yes," I agreed. "You can glance at God in your heart and it doesn't take a minute. You can just glance at Him with love—or with whatever you are feeling, and know that He knows and He loves you." The children nodded. "You say these things so well. Now we come to the hard part.

"We talked about praying as being with God and giving Him a tour of our heart. We want His help and His blessing. We want Him to go on loving us. We want to be happy. Does everybody agree?" Everybody did. The older children began to look a little puzzled, a little wary. They seemed to suspect something was coming. They were right.

"I want us to think about Jeremiah the prophet for a while. In the Hebrew Scripture there is a book named after Jeremiah. He was a man who was very special to God. God asked him to do some hard work and to tell the people what He—God—wanted the people to do. They didn't always like what Jeremiah told them. Sometimes they were very mean to Jeremiah. They beat him up; they even threw him down a well that had dried up and left him there to die. (His friends helped him out of the well later.) Still Jeremiah stayed faithful to God, although he complained. I don't really blame him for complaining, do you?" They didn't.

"You know that God always, always knows best. After all, He is our Creator. He made us. He gave us everything we have including *ourselves*. Truly He knows what makes us happy, and that is what He wants for us all the time. We have a hard time trying to figure it out sometimes, but God always knows. We make mistakes and sometimes have to do things over. That happens to you, doesn't it?"

"Oh, yes." There wasn't a person in the room disagreeing, including the other teachers. "Since God's the only one who never makes a mistake, we have to expect to make them. Well, one day God wanted to teach Jeremiah something. He really wanted to make a point, so instead of just telling him what was on His mind, He told Jeremiah to go to the potter's house. How many of you have ever seen pottery being made?"

Much to my surprise, more than half of the children had seen a potter work. A large number of them had worked on a wheel themselves. This city has a good art center which works at making things available to ordinary people. Some of the teachers told me they had used filmstrips with the children about pottery.

"Will those who know something about pottery tell the others who haven't been to the art center or didn't see the filmstrip?"

"Well, there's this wheel."

"How do you turn it?"

"With your feet."

"Why do you use your feet?"

"Well, maybe you could get an electric one."

"Maybe you could. But why use your feet?"

"Because your hands are busy."

"Good! Busy doing what?"

"Working the clay." They went on to say how the potter throws the clay on the wheel. A few knew that the clay is thrown to get the air bubbles out, to purify it, so it will hold together better. They all knew that the clay had to be centered, and that the potter raised it with the pressure from his or her hands.

"Did you ever notice anything about the potter's hands?"

"They are very muddy and dirty." Ronnie said right away.

"They sure are!" I agreed. "Anything else?"

"He wets the clay a lot, to keep it wet. It's important to keep it wet or it will crumble away."

"Good point! Does anyone know anything else about how the potter's hands work?" One child did.

"I tried it," Elsie remembered. "It's hard to keep it even. You put one hand inside and one hand outside and try to keep it even.

If you don't and put too much pressure on one side, it will make a hole."

"Yes, that is quite so. Those of you who have raised a pot, does it always come out the way you want it to?"

They laughed and said, "No. Hardly ever."

"Does it come out so that you can use it?"

"Sometimes. Then you can decorate it too, and make it look pretty."

"Well, you do know a lot," I said to them. "You knew much more than I had expected you to. What I want to do now is go back over the story. God told Jeremiah to go to the potter's house and watch the potter work. Jeremiah watched the potter do all the things that you just said. Then God reminded Jeremiah that when the pot, or bowl or vase—or whatever it is that the potter is making—doesn't come out right, the potter does what?"

"Squishes it down and starts all over," giggled Emmy.

"And over, and over, and over and over . . . 'til you wonder if it ever will come out right." added Bert.

"You sound like you've had experience," I said to him.

"Yes, lots. My dad does pottery and I hang around."

"Well, here's the punch line. Ready?" God said to Jeremiah, "As the clay is in the potter's hands, so are you in Mine." Will you say that after me. "As clay is in the potter's hands, so are you in Mine." The children did.

"Let's look at what that might mean. The potter throws the clay—don't we say sometimes in our lives that something 'throws us?' Maybe we say, 'it throws us for a loop!' When we say that, generally it's about something we found very surprising. Sometimes it's something we don't like much. The potter throws clay to get the air out, not that air is bad, but it's bad for the clay if we want it to hold together. Sometimes things happen to us, we don't like them, but God lets them happen to get the air bubbles out— the things which might cause us harm, although we might not recognize it at the time.

"Then the potter begins to make whatever it is that is to be made. An interesting thing is that the word used in the Hebrew Scripture for *making* the pot is the same word that is used in the beginning of the Bible, in Genesis, for God's *making* the world. It's a serious word, this *making* is. If the potter is careful to make a good pot, God is so much more careful in making us, don't you think?"

"Then you said that the potter keeps wetting the clay to keep it moist, so it doesn't fall apart. We talked about water before. Does anyone remember?"

They remembered the woman at the well, and the living water, and Jesus saying to ask for the living water.

"Does anyone know what water is a symbol of?"

"Faith." "Yes, indeed. Why do you think we use the symbolism of the potter wetting the clay?"

"We need to keep getting—gee, it sounds dumb to say, but like—wet with faith so we will live the way God wants?"

"Yes, that's right. That's another reason we need to pray every day. Like the clay which needs to be kept moist, we need God to keep our spirits well. It's that fountain within which we talked about with Jesus and the woman at the well. Just as the clay is centered on the wheel, we need to be centered with God. How do you suppose we do that?"

"By having God in our heart!"

Before I could say more a child asked, "What about that part about when it doesn't turn out right?" Paula, a serious fifth grader seemed worried.

"What did the potter do?" I asked.

"He started it over."

"Sure. What do we do when we make mistakes?"

"We start over. How many times do we have to do that?"

"How many times do we need to? That's how many. It's OK with God, so I guess it should be OK with us. Don't you think so?"

Most of the children did. Some weren't so sure. The sixth grade boys, especially, were quite sure they did not like the idea. They did not like thinking of themselves as clay in God's hands. They did not like that at all, not one iota. Some got angry at the thought.

"The Bible doesn't say anything about the potter saying the clay is bad, and he doesn't throw it out. He just starts over and works it into another bowl or pot. The same with God and us. When we make mistakes and start to come out like lopsided people, God's hands re-shape our clay. The really nice part is that His hands are loving, and we know He will make us better."

Most of the children seemed content with the thought of this, but not the sixth grade boys. I left them stewing and began the slides.

Karen, a friend of mine, is a fine potter. Several weeks earlier she had allowed me to photograph her at work: studio, wheel, clay, water, the kiln, vessels fired and some not yet baked. When we come to those slides we had to talk about the kiln—about the very high temperature, and the glaze which seals the vessel and allows it to hold liquids safely. With the older children I discussed being tried, how no one is a fully mature and happy adult who hasn't gone through fire somehow, and come out stronger than before. Some looked as if they understood. It was enough, I thought, if the notion gets planted in them. Someday, I hoped, it would come back to mind. However, the sixth grade boys still were having nothing to do with it.

When I did this session with the children's parents, there was a potter among them. Catherine affirmed all that had been said and added another note. "In any other art form, something comes between the artist and the work," Catherine said. "Only in pottery is there nothing between the artist's hands and the clay. There's no brush, no chisels, no molds. The artist's hands work directly with the clay." How true of God and us!

In the prayer room I invited the children to get as comfortable as possible, breathe gently, and welcome God in their hearts. "Give Him a tour . . . then let Him know from you what you think of Jeremiah's story. If you like the idea of God's hands lovingly forming you, and helping shape you into a good and happy human being, be aware of it. If the idea pleases you, or angers you, or you feel resentful, or you feel comforted, be aware of it. Whatever you feel is what you feel. Let God know from you what this Bible story means to you."

After a few moments I added, "Now do be quiet a moment and listen in case God wants to let you know something. He might want to talk to you now; He might wait until later. At some time He will. Let's take a moment, in case the time is now."

After a few minutes (two probably are enough, if you are watching a clock): "Think of all the people who love you and whom you love. Put them all into your heart. You and God look at them together and love them together. If something special is going on

102

with any of them, let God know from you. Then love them together some more."

Allow several minutes to pass, then say: "Now remember God
always is loving you. No matter how you feel about being like clay
in His hands, no matter what you do or don't do, He does love you.
Let go of everything else now—it will all sort out—and just enjoy
God's loving you, for He truly does."

At the end I reminded them that they can do this anytime, any
place, with whomever they chose—just as Jesus prayed anytime,
with anyone. All we need is to take a moment to remember God
is with us, loving us; and receive His loving us as the earth does
rain. Then I asked the children to open their eyes, sit up slowly
and spend a minute with themselves. We concluded with the prayer
that Jesus taught us to pray.

Before the seventh grade left they told me they had a surprise
for me. They looked very pleased with themselves. Their teacher
picked up his guitar and indicated that the students break into
what were obviously prearranged groups. Jim plucked a chord and
the children began a round:

> *Love, love, love, love*
> *it is the Christian call.*
> *Love your neighbor*
> *as God loves us all.*

They sang well and with relish. I was surprised and charmed by
the way they sang. At that point the school principal passed the
door. We invited Mary Ann in and the class sang the round over
again. It was the best ending of a prayer session ever. Everybody
left pleased and some humming.

In Summary

About Prayer in General

1. There's no ONE BEST posture: do what suits your prayer that
   day.
2. Open eyes or closed; do what suits your prayer that day.
3. Pictures, music may help or distract; do what suits your prayer
   that day.

About Jesus' Prayer

1. at different times, in different places
2. with many different people
3. for all sorts of human needs

About Our Prayer

1. at different times, in different places
2. with many different people
3. for all sorts of human needs
4. reviewing the day with God in our heart, being as clay in His potter's hands—for He made us, loves us, yearns for our happiness

Be Aware

God *is* with us always!

Enjoy each other!

Chapter 10

After You Talk to God, Who Do You Talk to about God?

(And Other Questions from the Children)

"After you talk to God, who do you talk to about God? . . . God again?"

Two frustrated fifth graders had looked tentatively into my office, and at a nod from me bounded in and plopped into the empty chairs. Without preamble, that is how Angie started.

"After you talk to God, who do you talk to about talking to God? . . . God again?" She didn't like her own question or answer, and she was frustrated.

"Do you have the same concern?" I asked Elaine. Nodding affirmatively she added, "If I told any of my friends, they'd think I was crazy."

"Have you tried talking to someone?"

Angie said that she had. "My brother and I are pretty good friends. I told him and he just laughed. I felt stupid. I told my mom and she just said, 'Yes, Yes,' and kept making dinner. Who do you talk to?"

"What about each other?" The girls looked startled.

"You've shared enough between you to know you have the same questions." Yes, they had.

"You both had God in your hearts enough to know what that's like—at least so far." Yes, they had.

"You know good things are going on, and still it is different enough that you want to check it out; or it's good enough that it makes you glad, and you want to tell someone; or perhaps it's not working this time, and you wonder why." That was so, but no spark was struck. "Now you say you need to talk to someone about it."

The questions, as their articulated needs, don't surprise me. What continuously surprises me is how young the children are who are aware of these things. How clearly they ask for validation of their experiences! I am touched by them.

"You are asking me very grown-up questions," I told them. "It's easier to find a good dentist or a good doctor to help you than to find a good friend who is willing to talk to you on that level of life. I am impressed that you realize it and am happy that you are willing to come here and talk about it. Now let's think about it together. Why do you think it is hard to find someone to talk to after you've talked to God?"

Elaine started. "You know what you want to say, but it's hard to say it . . . say it exactly. And you're always afraid of being laughed at."

Angie picked up. "I don't think my brother ever prayed like this. He laughs when he isn't sure. If he didn't do it, he doesn't know what it's like."

She thought a minute, brightened, and then softly confided, "I pray for my brother. I don't tell him because I'm afraid he'll laugh. My mom told me he really wants to go to this dance in his school, but he's afraid to ask a girl. He plans to ask this girl and I'm praying that she says yes. It would be awful for him if she didn't. But, I'm not telling him I'm praying for him."

"Why not?"

"We used to tease each other a lot. We don't do that any more, but . . . I guess we could start it again."

"You could. You might. You don't have to. You know what I wonder?" Both girls looked at me. "I wonder if you and your brother don't feel some of the same things. Here you are saying that you don't know who to talk to after you talk to God, and that's a real concern. Here you are saying, too, that you pray for your brother and you don't tell him. I wonder if you watched for the right time— not when he's in a rush or when his friends are around—I wonder if you couldn't tell him? And if the girl should say, no, that it's her loss because you know him and how great he is?"

Angie pondered that one. "Do you have a brother?"

"I do."

"Are you friends?"

"Joe and I are good friends."

"Do you do things together, even now when you are grown-up?"

"Sure we do."

"Like what?"

"Come over here," I myself went to a far wall in my office. Hanging there is a photograph I took of my brother, Christmas week. We had spent a day walking on the beach. While I changed the film in my camera, Joe stood quietly looking at the ocean. When the camera was loaded, I photographed him that way, in a typical pose watching the waves come.

"Even though we are both grown-up, any chance we get, we go to the beach and walk for hours. Sometimes we talk. Sometimes we just walk together and enjoy the ocean and each other's company. I hope that's the way it works out for you and your brother."

Angie hoped so, too.

"Back to your first question. Wanting to talk to someone after you talk with God is a very good thing. I hope you find someone. At different times in your life it will be different people. Not everyone will understand—you are perfectly right. Besides, that is a very special and private part of your life—you have to be careful that you find a right person to trust. It is also worth all the effort you put in to it. Many, many people who are serious about their relationship with God search for someone to talk to about it. You are very welcome to come in here and talk to me. You might want to talk to your teacher. Maybe Father John or Father Steve. Who else might you think about?"

"I know! My grandpa!" she was beaming.

"Good. That sounds like a really fine idea. You do that and remember that you might want to do this most of your life. When you do, there are always people you can find, but you might have to search a bit, alright?"

On their way out Angie took a deep breath and then shyly said: "There's one more thing I want to tell you . . . I pray in a tree I climb. You know what I do?" I didn't.

"I have a pretty blue cup. I put flowers into it and put it on the branch with me, right up against the tree trunk. That's what I look at when I pray." Angie's friend grinned and so did I. The two girls left.

Other children choose to come to my room alone. One of them started with, "Can I tell you how I pray at home?" "Of course you may. I'd like to hear that. . . ."

"Last year for Christmas my grandma gave me a book of Bible stories," Jim told me. "Every night I go to bed and read one story. Then I think about it until I fall asleep." He looked very satisfied and waited for a response.

"You know what I hope?" I asked him.

"What?"

"I hope you do that for a long, long time to come. Do you think you might?"

"Oh, yes, I like it! Sometimes, the next day I tell my little brother the story I just read."

"Do you know what I hope?" I asked a second time.

Jim laughed. "You hope I keep it up for a long, long time!"

"Smart! . . . Now get back to your class!" He skipped out.

Alex wasn't so easy. He's a bright boy, recently transferred into the school. With unusual dignity for a seventh grader, he formally asked to see me. Then his woes poured out. At first I thought his concern was perceived hypocrisy of his step-mother's and his father's social manners. On impulse I asked him if he had ever been in therapy.

"Child guidance," he corrected me. I believed it. He knew all the jargon and used it fluently. At one point I couldn't bear his complaining and his scenarios any longer.

"Shh!"

Alex jumped.

"Shh! Be quiet!"

"But I'm not finished."

"Shh!"

He was an obedient child—disgruntled, but obedient.

"Close your eyes, Alex. Don't look at anything. Turn your mind off."

His eyes popped open. "How do I do that?"

"Close your eyes and breathe slowly and deliberately. Breathe slowly and rythmically . . . slowly and rythmically."

His breathing fell into an easy pattern. "Keep breathing that way. Gently let one thing you want most surface. Gently. A few things might bubble up. Look at them in peace. When the most important one comes you will know it. Gently."

The boy began to weep—quietly, miserably.

"Do you want to tell me what the one thing is, or do you want to keep it to yourself? It's perfectly all right with me either way. Tell me what you want."

His eyes opened, still wet. "I want to tell you. What I want is . . ."

The sobs took over.

"Take your time."

"What I want is to be absolutely sure, absolutely sure that . . ."

The sobs took over again. His voice rose in pitch, high and thin. Mingled with sobs, "that . . . somebody . . . loves . . . ME."

I put some Kleenex close to him and waited. "Take your time. It's OK."

"How can you be absolutely sure that someone loves you? Aside from God, of course."

We talked about the people he loves—and did he love them the same day by day? These *are* the people he loves. Absolutely? Well . . . there are days. Alex had the grace to grin.

"You know, Alex, there is only one God. You don't have the job. Nor do your mom or dad or sister or stepmother. So we are all imperfect and uneven. Uneven in how much we love uneven in how much we show it. I don't know how human beings can do better. I know *I* don't. Do *you?*" He didn't either. Might he allow the same unevenness to his parents? That took awhile. Then he cocked his head to the side, smiled ruefully and thought he might. He asked for one last Kleenex and could he come back sometime? He could indeed (and did), but he wasn't leaving quite yet.

"I'm not?"

"No, you're not because we aren't finished yet. What I want you to do, sometime today, is to spend time with God quietly. Put into your heart your family *and* your stepmother (he made a face). You and God look at them together. Then you be quiet and see what happens. Are you willing to do that? Unenthusiastically, he was. Maybe you'd rather talk to your youth minister about it—you're close to Dick, aren't you? Maybe you'll want to keep it to yourself awhile. But do be with God and your family." He promised he would and left.

After class two boys lingered behind the others. They both looked quite woe begone . . . unusual for these ten year olds.

"What's the matter?" I asked.

"My best friend is moving away." Harry poked the other little boy.

"He's my best friend."

"Where are you moving to?" I asked Nick.

"Just to another school," he answered. "My father wants me to go to an all boys school . . . I'm gonna miss Harry."

The two of them used their shirt sleeves to wipe away the tears.

Harry went on, "My dad said he'd drive me to Nick's house so we can play together sometimes. And we are in the same class in the art center, but . . . it isn't the same."

"No, it isn't. Nor will it be."

Their class had left.

"Thank you for telling me this boys. Nick, I shall miss you too. Not so much as Harry will because you and Harry are such good friends, but I shall miss you. If you are ever in the neighborhood please feel free to come in and use the prayer room. Will you?"

Nick said he'd like that. I asked Harry to come and see me after Nick left. That is, if he wanted to.

Harry wanted to. Several days later he appeared in the depths of gloom. "I miss Nick," was all he could say. Tears wet his cheeks.

"I believe you. Tell me, Harry, is it worth it?"

He looked bewildered.

"You and Nick grew to be great friends. Now you are separated, and you're too young to drive so you don't get to visit as often as you'd like. You have the pain of separation."

"Why do you ask if it is worth it?"

"Because love costs. When you love someone dearly you re-ceive much—but it costs. Looking at your friendship with Nick, your love is costing you pain now. Is his friendship worth it?"

"Yes!" There was no hesitation.

"Good!" I was hoping you'd say that, and I'm glad you did."

"But I still miss him."

Poor boy!. . . and rich boy. I had nothing else to say so I invited him to stay awhile there in the prayer room and keep me company.

Just over half of the eighth graders came back—more girls than boys.

"What's on your minds?" I asked.

Getting settled in was obviously the first thing. Since it was not the complete class, there were more than enough pillows to go around. The boys smirked and smiled themselves into very comfortable "couches."

Finally one of them asked, "We were talking about how God can't be good. Look at all the stuff in the newspapers and on TV."

"What stuff do you dislike the most?"

"Drought," said Jim.

"Wars," insisted Susy. "My oldest brother died in a war."

"Where people don't have enough to eat—like those pictures of little kids with big stomachs, but you can see the bones in their chests."

"Endangered species. I don't want any animal to go out of existence."

"The way some people live—like when they don't have anything nice."

"That's quite a list. You're right, these are bad things, things which cause much pain and suffering in a world like ours. With all the science and technology at our command you'd think these things wouldn't have to be." They agreed. . . . "But they are." They agreed again.

"What you are touching on is sin; not necessarily personal sin, like when you deliberately do something wrong, but the sin of our society—the things we do as a people or a nation that are not in keeping with the great commandment to love God with all we are and to love our neighbor as ourself. Can anyone name one thing that might be a social sin?

There was a long pause. Finally, Jerry spoke up. "I heard my dad and my uncle talking about world hunger, you know, all those kids like John said with big stomachs and the bones on their chests almost sticking out."

"Yes."

"Well, my Uncle George was saying what good farm lands we have in this country and how much of them are not being used in order to keep the prices right. I don't understand it, but it doesn't seem right to me if we *can* grow the food that we don't send some to people who don't have any."

"What do you think you can do about it?"

"Hey, I'm a kid! What can I do? People don't pay any attention to kids."

"It's true that very few people get to do anything spectacular. What's ordinary that you can do?"

They seemed puzzled. Was it enough that they recognized the world's ills? I thought not and told them so. I told them we have responsibilities as Christians and as citizens of our nation as well as inhabitors of the earth. Aside from the natural disasters (like the drought), most of the things they said came about from people's decisions. We are people; we are able to make decisions.

Larry began, "I guess I look for someone else who's doing something and see if I can help."

"Good, we are getting started! Can you give me an example?"

"The youth group in my church worries about hungry people. Almost all our kids are volunteering this summer to help out in the soup kitchen. There's a lot of work to do, and our leader is planning that out now."

"We're going to high school next year. Maybe in high school we can learn more about how the laws are passed, and maybe we can get better ones passed."

"How might you go about that?"

"Like this youth group. If we could get some kids together and help the grown-ups who are doing things, that would be something."

"Yes, it would be. Volunteering your time and energy to help with something you believe in is important."

"So's giving money," added Tim.

"Yes, that is also important. Much good is done because of generous financial contributions. In addition to that, however, it is important to involve your person. I hope, at different times in your lives, you will volunteer your selves to some cause that you believe in.

"You can't do everything," sighed Ro. I had the feeling she was imitating someone.

"You can't, but you can do something. When we pray to God in our hearts some of you might show Him your concerns and ask Him for help to decide which one to get involved in. Also decide what it is you might be able to do, whether it be helping out more, studying more, volunteering or just finding people who are willing to be involved . . . however, you are able."

"You know," Dave said, "when I come here I think about things I never thought about before." Some of the others agreed. I was pleased.

"Have you any other questions for today?" They didn't. I did.

"I'm asking this for my own information. Do you talk about the prayer room to your friends?"

They said they did, but only to their friends in this school, not to anyone else.

"That's okay with me," I assured them, "but it would be helpful to me to know why you don't." I waited.

"Well, it's really personal when your mind goes that free. . . ."

"It's hard to understand if you didn't do it. . . ."

"They wouldn't know what I was talking about if I said I had God in my heart. . . ."

". . . I wouldn't try it with anyone who didn't have the experience. . . ."

Again and again these children surprised me. They were so aware of the importance of experience, at least in this context. (Of course they don't want to hear of their lack of experience when they want to try other things!) As with the other youngsters who asked, who do you talk to after you talk to God, I encouraged them to be selective in their choice of a confidant . . . but not to give up the search for someone who also takes God very seriously and has a conscious relationship with Him.

In the quiet prayer at the end of the session, after they had time to welcome God into their hearts, I suggested an additional part of the usual "tour."

"Go over the TV newscasts and the newspaper reports which bother you. Hunger, drought, war, endangered species, whatever it is that upsets you. Show these reports to God. Let Him know how you feel about whatever issues bother you most. Explore with

God in your heart what your responsibilities might be as an eighth grader in the United States of America. Put into your heart all the people who love you and whom you love. Add those you are concerned about—those suffering from hunger or drought or whatever issues touch you—put them into your heart, too. You and God look at them together and love them together. What might your love for them mean? What might 'Love your neighbor as yourself' mean for these people and you?" (I never ask them to share this part of the prayer out loud. I still think it gives them more freedom and more likelihood for development when they are not asked to articulate).

"Let the people fade and remembering God always is loving you, enjoy His delight in you." At the end I reminded them that they can do this any time, any place. For this prayer all they need is them*selves* . . . no money, no talent, no test scores, no equipment—just their own heart's willingness to receive God's love for them. They sat up slowly, and we concluded as usual with the Lord's Prayer.

A seventh grade contingent came in—all boys. They had made the best nests and couches out of pillows. (If it's not the whole class, I close an eye to the "one pillow" rule.) When they were ready I asked them to close their eyes and in the privacy of their minds and hearts answer the question, "Why did you come today?" And then, "Why did you *really* come today?" Then, "If you *really* told the truth, why did you come?" By now most of them were laughing. "To get out of class," "to get away from girls. . . ." Then they stopped laughing and added, "for some peace and quiet," "to relax," "to have some quiet time with God."

They had no questions. They had gotten there without girls, and it seemed that was as far as their plans had taken them. "You know the rule," I told them. "I don't prepare for small volunteer groups. You tell me what you would like to do and choose something which is appropriate for the prayer room."

Johnny said he'd like to do a phantasy; we hadn't done any in a while. The others looked eager. I agreed.

"Make yourselves as comfortable as you want, but stay alert." All of the boys snuggled into pillows on the floor. "Attend to your breathing. As other thoughts come, allow them and acknowledge them. Let them go. Just breathe. . . .

"Now imagine yourself on a camping trip with a few of your friends. The day is very beautiful. It's your favorite season of the year, and the weather is just right. You decide to stop hiking and make camp early to enjoy the day. You and your friends make camp. You look around and think you'd like to climb a small mountain nearby. Nobody wants to go with you so you go off alone.

"First you walk through the meadow. There's a path through the trees. You follow it. You don't even mind being alone as you listen to the birds and the small animal sounds. Then suddenly you become aware you forgot something. What did you forget? . . . What do you do about it?

"As you walk higher and higher up the mountain the trees start thinning out and the ground gets rockier. The path turns into a ledge. It is wide enough not to be dangerous, but you have to cross it to get to the top.

"When you're about half way along the ledge a mountain goat jumps down the slope and stands right in your way. You need to get past the mountain goat. You will. What do you do?

"Well, you get by the goat, finish crossing the final part of the ledge and climb to the top of the mountain. Someone had told you that there was an interesting cave at the top of the mountain. You go looking for it. When you find it there are two monsters guarding it. What do you do about it? . . .

"You succeed in passing the monsters and get into the cave. Look around. Explore it . . . you will find a box in the cave—a box with your name on it. . . . Open the box. Take out what it contains and look at it. . . . What might it mean to you?"

"Let the phantasy fade, come back to this room, this time and the rest of us here . . . sit up, stretch, and yawn if you want."

I instructed them to tell the phantasy to two other boys. There was a lot of laughing. When I pulled the group together, I asked them:

"What did you forget?"

Mostly the answers were knives, ropes, compasses, maps, a jacket, a water canteen. One said, "girls." All laughed.

"What did you do about it?" They were a good crowd. Nobody blamed anybody. All of them decided to make the best of it and go on anyway. They were resourceful and confident, these boys.

"What about the mountain goat?" Seventh grade boys! They did things like: stabbed him; grabbed his horns and twisted his head off; threw him over the ledge; cut off his head. All of this was said with many gestures and much pride.

"What about the monsters at the mouth of the cave?" There was much more of the same thing. Here, though, several had distracted them with food. One had made friends with the monsters.

"This is serious," I told them. "I want you to think with no kidding, no sharing. Think inside yourself: if you had to put a real person's name on the goat and real peoples names on the monsters guarding the cave, whose names would you put on them? You need three names." Some of the boys understood immediately. Some looked puzzled.

"Of course, the goat and the monsters stand for real people who get in your way when you want to do something. They are real people who have some authority over you. Let it come . . . you do know! Who are they? Intelligence dawned on every face.

"I don't want you to say this out loud. And I don't want you to joke about this part, either. It's too important for you. Think of how you treated the goat and the monsters in your phantasy. You feel very strongly, don't you? For boys of your age, that is expectable. It's OK. There are two things which are important: one is that you recognize the strong feelings that you have, probably stronger than you've ever felt in your life . . . it looks like you've done that." They looked very serious and agreed.

"The second thing is that once you recognize that that's how you *feel,* you need to decide how you are going to *act.* Now in real life you aren't going to throw people over the ledge or stab them or chop off their heads—not physically. The boys were smiling. "How are you going to come to terms with those strong and violent feelings, and how will you act? That's something to think about and pray about and maybe talk to your parents or some relative or older friend who has gone through it already." They nodded.

"What did you find in the cave?"

Some had wishes come true, a fine knife, some sports equipment. One found a lovely family picture. Almost all found ordinary things. Almost all were things which connected them with their family. I pointed that out. "If the goat or the monsters represented someone in your family, pay attention to what you found in the box in the cave. It might show you how much you really care." Several of the youngsters looked relieved. "Growing into young manhood is exciting, but it's very hard sometimes, too. Does anyone want to say anything?" No one did.

Quiet prayer time followed. (I always use the same general format. Talking to the teachers reinforced my decision to do just that. The regularity of it and the expectable format allows for a degree of comfort and for the insertion of the stuff of the day.)

"Welcome God to your heart . . . give Him a tour of what is going on . . . show God, in any way you want, your phantasy. Go over with Him how you got past the mountain goat and the monsters . . . tell Him the names you put on those three creatures and spend some time with God about how you feel about those three people. . . . Listen, in case God wants you to understand something now.

"Put into your heart everyone who loves you and whom you love . . . pay special attention to the three people whom the animals represented . . . you and God look at them together; let God know anything further you have to communicate to him about those three people. . . . Now you and God love them together.

"Let the people fade, and you and God be alone together. Remember, He made you good and always He loves you, no matter what you do or don't do, no matter how you feel or don't feel. Just be quiet and enjoy God's loving you.

"Remember, too, you can do this whenever you want. All you need is your own self. Now open your eyes, sit up slowly, and spend a minute alone with yourself and what this all might mean to you.

We ended with the Lord's Prayer. On the way out Tommy burst out, "That was neat!" It really was.

When a group of fourth graders came in, some among them were excited by an every-night-for-a-week telecast they were watching. "Why do you like Leo Buscaglia so much?" I asked them. Fourth graders were very definite.

"He's honest . . . he's open to you . . . he says: 'Let go, have a purpose!' He lets you know how he feels about things . . . you can trust him . . . he's a great guy." It was easy to talk to them about what that might mean for the way they live and treat people.

The fifth graders who came were caught up in how you can listen to God. Well, listening wasn't exactly the problem . . . how do you *hear* God, was the real question. "Does he use a voice?" I asked how many ever heard a voice. Not one. "Then how do you hear God?" I pressed.

Long silence.

Finally Trudy said, "You just know. You know, you know. It's different from knowing other things."

"Yeah," Ben added, "all sorts of things kind of go across your brain, but when it's the right one you know. Like she said," he paused. "You never know when it's gonna happen."

Amen!

Children and teachers both fill in the schedule I have hanging on the outside of the prayer room door. They keep coming with very human things: divorces, relationships with friends, popularity, peer pressure. (There's not so much concern with drugs as there is with shoplifting, a dozen junior high students told me. It's fun to see if you're smart enough not to get caught. "And later?" I asked. "Well, that's why we came. . . .")

"How do you make friends with a girl you really like, when the other kids can't stand her, and you don't want to lose your other friends, either?" Values, choices, integrity: Young children are so aware of them perhaps not by name, but in their context.

"When it comes to stringing your beads at night, what do you wish you had done? . . . How much are you willing to suffer to live what you say you believe? . . . What is really the most important choice for you, and are you willing to live with the consequences of it?" . . . Children can imagine themselves into consequences of choices.

No matter what their experience, it fits the prayer. "Show God what is going on—particularly . . . Put people into your heart, especially . . ." (Lastly, and no matter what was resolved well or poorly, or not resolved at all): "Enjoy God's loving you." Often I think things are not settled then and there, but there is a start—a start with the door wide open because the ending of the prayer is enjoying God's delight in His people: you.

In Summary

Questions

No matter the question or concern:

1. Listen.
2. Validate, affirm as is appropriate.
3. Explore, if it seems fruitful.
4. No matter what the content, put it into the context of prayer:
   - Invite God into your heart.
   - Show Him what is going on in your life, especially . . . (whatever is being discussed).
   - Spend time with God in your heart about this.
   - Give time for listening.
   - Put into your heart the people you love, and the people concerned in the context of the discussion.
   - Listen again, if you are to do something with or for the others.
   - Always end enjoying God's loving you.

Be Aware

No matter the stuff of the day
   the questions
   the concerns

It all,
all of it,

is a starting point for prayer:
   for putting it before God
   for listening
   for responding

Chapter 11

(But You ARE, Aren't You?)

More of the teachers were telling me the students wanted to come to the prayer room outside of class time. I was willing to see them individually, or in small groups, or with a friend (as with Angie and Elaine), as long as I was in the building and they were having a free period. (Children can become very prayerful when there is a science or math test scheduled.) I did not see them unless the classroom teacher arranged the group for us.

When the children came apart from the full class I prepared no session or visuals for them. The agenda was their responsibility. By and large, it was productive.

Eighth grade Jane's mother died. Last year her 16-year-old brother died. Both of them died from cancer. The teacher came to my room. "The kids are off the wall," she told me. "They're so upset about this. If you have a free space today do you think it would help for them to come down to the prayer room?"

"I'll make the time, but please make sure that those who come *choose* to come—OK?"

An hour later about three-quarters of the class came to the prayer room. When I take the children outside of class I sit in a different place. It took them a moment to rearrange themselves. They were very quiet, almost—I thought—tinged with a certain animosity.

"Make yourselves comfortable. Now close your eyes and remember where you were when you heard Jane's mother died. Remember who told you and what you were doing. This next part is very important. Let yourself feel how you were feeling when you realized what had happened."

I waited a few minutes. A few tears came from under closed eyes. "Really feel how you felt."

For a minute I debated inside myself. These eighth graders were not known for sharing in front of the class. I decided this was too important; I would not give them an option today. They had come on their own initiative and I would prod them.

"Take what you were feeling and translate those feelings into adjectives. Now open your eyes. I am going to go around the group (there were about 15 youngsters there), and everyone is going to say out loud one feeling you felt. Please use *adjectives*.

"Jim, you start."

"Depressed."

"Like crying."

"Glad it wasn't my mom. Then guilty because I felt glad."

By the end of this part of the meeting virtually every youngster had said the same thing—"glad it wasn't my mom; guilty because I felt glad."

"Mad. What did Janie do to deserve this?"

"Sorry for Janie and her dad."

"Angry."

"I was angry too . . . it isn't fair."

"Sad."

"I got so furious with God, then I got scared. It was God I was mad at!"

Some repeated what others said. Most of the children looked and sounded depressed.

"It really bothers you, doesn't it? I'm glad you're willing to recognize this and come to the prayer room. This is one healthy way to deal with it."

"Healthy?" Kenny confronted me. "What would be an unhealthy way?"

"When you're in pain, knowing the pain is a good thing. Hiding from it doesn't do anything to deal with it, and it hurts us besides."

"Hide how?"

"Ignore, pretend it's not there . . . drink, get drunk . . . take drugs—then you'll fry your brains for sure, causing your body harm."

Leo looked somewhat apologetic. "I don't think you can answer this, but I want to ask anyway. Why does God let it happen? How do we know there is a God anyway?"

"You're right. I can't answer that one because it's too important. Do the rest of you have the same question?" They sure did!

"I'll discuss that one after I ask another question. Who do you know who died?"

Most of the children had someone—grandparents, aunts, uncles, friends and, in one or two instances, parents.

"Then you know what it is like." A solemn acknowledgement from one. Another child said, "It happened when I was very small so I don't remember much." Some of the other children looked surprised and very thoughtful. Evidently they hadn't known of the deaths.

"And, Ed, your grandfather is very sick, isn't he?"

"Yes. Very."

"I want you to think very seriously. Think about all you know about yourself. Everything. How you feel, what you think, how you act. Is there anybody who knows everything, absolutely everything about you? God, maybe. No one else. Think of all the thoughts and feelings you've had ever since you came into the prayer room. Even if you could, if you tried telling someone all of them, what do you think your chances of success would be?"

"Not much," said Roger. "You'd be feeling all the time you were talking and so you wouldn't catch up unless you. . . ." he grinned, ". . . took time out for a nap."

"You're right. If you tried to tell someone everything about you, even for a day, you wouldn't have time for lunch! That's because we're so rich. (They looked very surprised at that.) Every human being is so rich in his or her own *self*. We are so rich in our feelings and knowledges and responses, there's no way anyone but God can possibly know them all. Sometimes we even surprise ourselves, don't we? If we are so rich in ourselves, then there is mystery in each of us, isn't there? It's not just information—like you didn't know Charley's father died when Charley was a little boy— it's what things like that do to a person." They understood that.

I went on, "Do you feel other people understand you completely? Really understand everything about you all of the time?" No one felt *that* understood!

"Again, part of the reason is that there is mystery in all of us. Sometimes we don't even understand ourselves too well or why we feel the way we do."

So far, so good. "Then there's another thought. You've been living 13 years or so ("Fourteen," growled one), and you have such riches and such mystery in your *self*. Now think of God. He's been living forever—literally forever. Is it any suprise that we don't know all about Him or understand Him completely? As there is mystery in us, there is infinitely more mystery in God. We want to believe in us, right? We need to believe in God, too. Do you remember the main virtues?"

"Faith, Hope and Love."

Mary Ellen added, "and the greatest of these is Love."

"Yes, the greatest is Love. That doesn't mean the others aren't great. Faith is difficult many times . . . that's why it rates among the top three. Believing in God and believing God truly loves us and made us to be happy takes a great deal of faith when we are suffering. When we are separated by death, that hurts a lot and we suffer." There was universal agreement to that.

"Then we have to make a decision. Do we choose to believe in God, hope and trust in Him? Maybe we have to pray like that man in the gospel, 'Lord, I do believe. Help my unbelief.' Sometimes that is the best we can do, and if that is so, it is good enough. Face it—we are creatures; we need to acknowledge mystery in our lives. I think it is a good thing to know there is someone bigger and better than we are; more powerful and truly loving. Sometimes we don't feel the comfort of it. Sometimes we might.

"The answer to your question, Leo, I think, is in terms of Faith and of mystery. It is not on the level of a math or a science problem. Life and death are far more precious, more important and more mysterious. Take some time to think about these things."

They were quiet. So was I.

After a bit Rosie said, "I don't want to go to the wake." Some of the others looked sympathetic. "The problem is, I don't know what to say to Jane."

That's real, I thought. "Let's get some help on that." I turned to the children who had been bereaved. "Are you willing to help your classmates and, through them, Jane?"

"Me?" blurted out Edith.

"Yes, you. When did your dad die?"

"Two years ago," she replied in a small voice.

"Are you willing to tell the others what helped you?" She was, but she found it hard to get started.

"What did people say to you?" The children were very attentive.

"They said all kinds of things . . . like how good my dad was . . . how they would miss him . . . how he was better off in heaven than being so sick on earth . . . I HATED IT WHEN THEY SAID THAT!"

"I bet you did. You missed him very much?"

"Yes," Edith continued. "Another thing I hated was when they said how good he looked in the coffin. He didn't. He didn't even look like himself."

"That's how I felt about my mother," I said. "I didn't think she looked like herself in the coffin." Edith nodded.

"Can you remember," I asked Edith because she seemed willing to go on, "what happened during the wake and those difficult days; can you remember what helped you?"

She thought a moment and then said, "People I really liked were there. I mean, they kept coming. Just that they came made me feel maybe I wasn't so alone."

"What about you?" I asked the youngster whose uncle had died.

"Yeah, that's right. It was really neat the way friends kept coming. Some of them brought food. We got to eat real good."

I turned to Theresa. "What about when your grandfather died?"

"I don't remember what people said very much. I liked it that they came and stayed with us. Like keeping us company."

Turning to the entire group I asked, "After listening to Edith, Ed and Theresa, what do you think the most important part of going to a wake might be?"

"Just being around for Janie and her Dad, I guess," said Sophie.

"Yes, don't underestimate how important *you* are and how important it is for Janie to know that she counts for something with you. Your being there is the best thing you can do for her. I hope you go. It isn't important what you say. Probably you don't have to say very much at all. Just let her know you care. That's the most important thing."

Edith agreed to that and said so. The others seemed to take her seriously. "I know there aren't clear cut answers to a lot of this—there is so much pain involved."

"Are there any more questions bothering any of you?"

After a brief hesitation Steve spoke up. "How do we treat Janie when she comes back to school? I mean . . . what do you do with a kid who's just lost her mom?"

Rosie said, "That bothers me, too. What do you do?"

"Edith?"

"When I came back, I wanted the kids to treat me the same as they always did. When they did, I was mad they didn't do something different . . . I don't know. . . ." her voice trailed off.

"I hope you are all listening to Edith," I said. "It's so hard to suffer a death of someone you love that you get all mixed up inside. You think you know what you want. If you don't get it, you're hurt; and if you get it, you don't want it. You want and want, and nothing satisfies or seems to help very much. Is that how it was with you, Edith?"

It was then she turned the table. "Did your dad die?"

"Yes."

"Is that how it was with you after he died?"

"That's how it was with me after my dad died. Yes."

A little silence.

"I still don't know what to do," came from Rosie.

"Do what comes," I suggested. "Make an effort to invite Janie to sit with you and go with you when you're going someplace. Try hard not to forget her. If she feels like the rest of us who have lost parents, she might not go with you. And maybe she won't even be nice about it. Then what?"

Rosie's look threw the question back to me. "Then what?"

"This is a very adult thing to say to you," I went on. *"Do what you do for your own sake.* So often people do things for other people with a sort of hook in it. For instance, if I invite you to my party then you'd better invite me to yours. Or if I give you something when I ask you, you'd better give me what I want. *Not so.* What you do, what you give, you do or give because that is the kind of person you are. You do it for your sake because it expresses your love, your generosity. It's nice if people respond well; of course, we'd all prefer that! If that's the only reason you do it,

126

don't do it! You'll find yourself living much more peacefully if you do what you do because that is how you keep the commandment of loving your neighbor as yourself. You love yourself enough to want to treat your neighbor, Janie, well—even if she is still hurting and so sorrowful that she can't respond. Now that is a lot to think about, and I hope it isn't too far above your heads. Is it?"

They were very sober. There didn't seem to be any more questions.

After a short pause, I invited them: "Lie down if you want. At any rate, make yourselves comfortable. I think it's time each of us spent some time with God. Welcome God into your heart. Let Him see how you feel about Janie and the deaths in her family. Now, in your heart go over with God all the things we said in the prayer room this morning, what that means to you and where your dissatisfaction or questions still are."

After a moment, "Be still; give God a chance." I waited longer, at this point, than usual. The children seemed very absorbed.

After a while, "Put into your heart all the people you love and who love you. This time include Janie and her family. You and God look at them together and love them together."

Again they stayed absorbed much longer than usual. I waited.

"Now let everyone else fade away, and let you and God be alone. Remember you can use words if you want or feelings or just be together. Do what suits you. Receive God's mysterious but real love for you." For the third time they stayed quiet longer than any time since I had been with them. Again I waited.

Finally, "Please open your eyes and sit up gently. Together, for ourselves and the people we love, for Janie and her family, let us pray the way Jesus told us to, 'Our Father. . . .' " They left very quietly.

I believe they were, as a class, very good to Janie.

In Summary

When There Is a Death

1. Gather the children.
2. Invite them to remember:
   when they heard about the death,
   where they were when they heard,
   how they were feeling about it.
3. Encourage them to say out loud (using adjectives) how they feel about it and:
   * Accept the expression of feelings as normal and natural.
   * Note anything particularly troublesome (perhaps making sure to see that child alone in the near future).
   * Deal with their questions on the spot.

The Wake

1. Identify the children present who have experienced death.
2. Ask if they are willing to tell the others what it was like for them; what helped them; what they did not like.
3. Invite the listening children to articulate what they heard, and give some thought to their own behavior at the wake.

Afterwards

When the bereaved child returns to school:

1. Again, let the children with experience speak to the point.
2. Again, let the listening children articulate what they understood.
3. Set the environment for them to expect:
   * the bereaved child's uncharacteristic behavior.
   * to give the bereaved child a long time and much consideration.
   * to have to extend a number of invitations before any might be accepted.

Be Aware

WHAT YOU DO
(for the bereaved child or for any other person)
DO FOR YOUR OWN SAKE
(because it expresses the kind of person you are)
for you, it is a
LIVING OUT
of the commandment
TO LOVE GOD, and
TO LOVE YOUR NEIGHBOR *AS YOURSELF*

Chapter 12
Puzzled Parents

(Are You Sure THIS Is Praying?)

A very lovely young woman was sitting right in front of me. The occasion was an evening of prayer in a neighboring parish. As the evening went on, the young woman looked a bit puzzled; then the expression on her face underwent some swift changes. It was so noticeable I stopped, and asked her if there was something she wanted to say.

"Now I know what Millie means!" She smiled, with waves of understanding still crossing her face.

"What does Millie mean?" I asked with curiosity.

"You're the Prayer Sister!"

Now the rest of the audience looked puzzled.

"At St. Augustine's we have a prayer room, and I spend time with the children and their teachers praying," I explained. Turning to the woman I asked, "Is Millie your little girl?"

"Yes. We belong to this parish, but there is no kindergarten here. My husband and I sent Millie over to St. Augustine's for kindergarten. She talks about God coming to her heart and wants me to do it with her. Now I know what she means."

Millie came skipping into my office the next morning holding her girlfriend's hand. "You met my mom!" she said. Then, one little foot curling inward, "We are going to pray together tonight."

The next time I met Millie's mom she told me how very active her five year old is. Generally when she put the child to bed she would lie down with her for a while to help quiet the child for sleep. Now when bed time comes, they welcome God in their hearts together, let Him know about the day; they name the people they love and love them together; then they pause to enjoy God's loving them. And that's how Millie now falls asleep. "At least, most of the time," her mother smiled.

We—the pastor, principal and I—had talked about involving parents in the prayer room. One of our ideas was to open it to the parents who wait for their children to be dismissed. Possibly I could be with them. As it turned out, there was neither the number nor the interest at that time. Occasionally someone comes in and is quiet or reads a bit. Generally, however, that is all that happens at 3 p.m.

During Advent we set up an evening of prayer for the parents. I explained what we do in the prayer room and did for them some sort of presentation on names and the name of Jesus. It went well.

It's hard, in these days of single-parent families and of both parents working families, to find a common good time. We never did. Our compromise was to vary the times so more people would be able to come some of the time.

One particular morning about twenty parents came. One father met me with "I can't stay for the whole meeting, but I shall sneak in periodically and observe the children." While I was inside myself, unsettled on what to do, I knew this did not sit well with me. "We'll have to talk about that, I think," I responded. He became angry. "It is my right as a parent." I still thought we had to think about it.

There is no furniture in the prayer room—just the large pillows the children like so much. All the parents but one sat on the pillows. They varied in ease and awkwardness. The one who had made the original statement stood next to and over me, arms folded. I could not see his face.

One thing I do know: when a group is serious, a group is responsible. These parents were serious. Some were skeptical; some were curious; all were interested.

I began, as I had during Advent, with the short history of the prayer room and a summary of what we do, promising that before the meeting was over I'd conduct a prayer experience with them similar to that which I do with their children. They agreed to that.

The big question, as both the parents and myself saw it, was: how can the parents who want to, be involved?

"I don't know the answer to that," I told them. There was an uneasy silence and some shifting of bodies on pillows. Perhaps we could start by my telling you my present opinion. It is by no means locked in concrete. Then we can discuss it and see what is to everyone's advantage." That seemed acceptable.

I told them that I recognize their right as parents, and I applaud their interest in their children's prayer. However, being with classes of children as I am, I really don't want other adults there. (There was a sharp intake of breath and a murmur of "Secrecy!" and "What's really going on?") The children get so involved in prayer that the thought of someone's *watching* is offensive to me, and I told them that. Besides, I make a very strong point that whatever they do, it is right. No performance is required. No grade is given. My fear is that, were parents present, some children would be inhibited; some would feel pressure to perform. Prayer is not a performance. On the other hand, I continued (very aware of the audible breathing of the gentleman standing next to and above me) that parents have every right to know about and, appropriately, participate in their children's education. My initial suggestion, for the sake of starting the discussion is this: parents are welcome as *participants* in prayer, but not as observers. That began it. The gentleman said little. Other parents said much. They talked about their experiences as den mothers and as scout leaders. From their own experiences they knew that children behave differently when there are visitors, particularly parents. But, some stuck, how do we know what is going on?

"Ask your children," I answered. "And ask their teachers."

"What do you mean, ask their teachers?"

Either I had failed to say it, or they had failed to hear it; I don't know which. This time they heard that teachers are present with their class. Not only are they present, but they are encouraged to follow up in any way they deem helpful.

"What happens if you notice something with a child? Will you call us?"

"No, I will not. What I do, and plan to continue doing, is confer with the teacher. When it seems advisable, the teacher will contact the parents. After all, the teacher is with the children five days a week and can give continuing help. Parents liked that.

"There's no crucifix in the room," one observed. To tell the truth, I had not myself noticed. We have several Bibles—children's versions, one with quality reproductions of Dali's works—in the room.

133

I had neglected to notice the absence of a crucifix. To several parents this was quite bothersome. To me, it was easily remediable. Some years ago I had been given a very beautiful gift. One of my friends, an artist, had made a crucifix for me. It is rough chunks of glass—ruby and amber—leaded together, with a lead corpus. When the sun strikes it, it makes puddles of amber and ruby colors on the floor and adjacent walls. I just moved it from my office window to the prayer room window. It shines beautifully through the plants and trees. Sometimes I watch a small child jockey for position into the color. "It's like church," one says. "It makes me feel holy." It seems to me to incorporate both death and resurrection.

We came back to the issue of parents' participation. One mother said thoughtfully, "When I hear my kids talking, I get jealous. I'm glad for them, but I want something for myself, too." Others heard that—and while they hadn't thought of it that way—hesitantly acknowledged their own wanting to pray more satisfyingly.

Another parent again brought up the difference in cub scouts when a parent comes in unexpectedly. That was easily assented to. The conversation seemed to be veering away from parents coming to the classroom. . . . One mother did not like that at all.

"How will we know—really know—what's going on?" Then she turned to me and ordered, "Sister, you must instruct the children to come home and tell us about their prayer, and what happened in their prayer time. That way I can be prepared to be a better mother."

For the moment I was nonplussed. Fortunately the pastor was present. With gentleness he turned to the woman. "Helen," he said, "That would be like having your mother-in-law along on the honeymoon!" She was miffed. The other parents were thoughtful.

"Thanks, John," I said to him. "That is what I was trying to say earlier. I think prayer is living a relationship with God. It is a special and unique relationship, because there is one God, one Creator of us all and each of us is His creature. God makes no carbon copies. However we experience His presence, it is our unique experience. Much of it, when we give our selves to it, is very difficult to articulate. Words almost tend to trivialize something which is quite sacred."

Turning to the parents I asked them to remember a time when they were very much in love, and made love with their spouses. After a moment I asked, "Thinking of those times of great love, and intense expression of your love for each other, could you have told anyone exactly what it was like? . . . even if you wanted to?" No, they couldn't. "That's how prayer, our living relationship with God, is.

"What you can do," I continued, "if you find another person who loves and is loved by his or her spouse, is say 'you know what it's like,' and the other person knows what it's like. When people have similar experiences, we know what it's like. We don't know the other person's experience from inside the other person." That seemed to make sense to them.

"In human experience," I went on, "we keep bumping into the phenomenon that what is most personal and private also is most universal. Still, it's each person's own joy and own pain. Those among us who have lost parents to death know what it is like. Yet, it is nuanced differently for each of us according to our own histories and personalities." They understood.

"That is true of your children, as well as of you and me. Their experience of God is equally true, equally valid, and equally difficult to share unless they meet someone who knows what it's like from experience. They won't have the language to describe what goes on in them. Nor are they at a developmental stage where they can catch hold consciously of their experience. Even the great mystics had trouble doing this—that's why they resorted to poetry. Some of them tried to express their experiences in frescoes or stained glass or other art forms. Language is inadequate. Imaginative forms let someone else who has had comparable experience say, 'I know.' If you pray, you can touch your child in this situation. If you don't, you won't."

"But I don't have the words," came the words painfully from one mother. "I get terrified of spontaneous prayer." Several other heads nodded affirmatively. This is so understandable to me. Spontaneous prayer, making up prayers, is not in our education or history. When suddenly confronted with it, having had few, if any, models and no practice, we go dumb. It's outside of what had been ordinary experiences. So they're ill at ease with spontaneous prayer.

I said things like this and then added, "Tell me the one best thing, very specifically, that is the *only* thing you do to make a good marriage. What is the one only way that covers every situation in which you communicate with your spouse." Other than saying something like "love," or "understanding," it's an impossible question.

"Why put those sorts of constraints on your relationship with God? There are endless ways of communications. Do what seems appropriate to the situation. The best part of being with God is that He always knows what we mean even if we don't say it well."

"We don't have much experience of that," Joan said. "We go to Mass, and we say the prayers we learned."

"True," I responded. "However, it is my guess that you all probably pray much more than you are aware of and give yourselves credit for. We can explore that if you want."

Finally one parent said: "I've been sitting here, thinking, all this time. Like the rest of you, I want to know what my children are doing. But I want something for myself, too. I wonder, Sister, if you'd be willing to take us parents separately?"

Her question really sparked interest. After some more conversation, this is what we decided. Parents would not come to the prayer room with the children for two reasons: It is disruptive to the children; parents want more.

We agreed that everytime I set up sessions for the seventeen classes, I'd call the president of the Parents' Association and set up a time for parents. She'd notify parents, with the principal's cooperation, by sending a notice home with the children. (The principal was most willing; the children did not always remember to deliver the note. One seventh grade boy muttered to me, "I'm not giving this to my parents. The prayer room is *mine!*" To accommodate parents, the principal asked the teachers to collect signed notes; that way we knew the parents knew about the time of the prayer session for them. It still meets with limited success.)

What the parents wanted is for me to do the same topic with them as I was doing with the children: use the same Scripture, the same music, the same slides. Content, however, was to be upgraded to adult level. That suggestion had total consensus (the standing gentleman had left to take care of a prior obligation.) And that is what we have been doing, with pleasure.

After the discussion I reviewed with the parents the content and Scripture I was using with the children, showed the slides, and encouraged them to be comfortable.

Every parent remained sitting on the pillows. I invited them to welcome God in their hearts and show Him (in words or in feelings or just by being together) what their life was like that day or that week. "Put today's discussion before God. Let Him know what it means to you, how it affects you. . . . Ask what He might want of you in this context . . . let Him know what you are willing to give Him. . . .

"Put into your heart everyone who loves you and whom you love, everyone about whom you are concerned. You and God look at them together. Let Him know from you what is special with each one: birthdays, anniversaries, illnesses, engagements, whatever—and ask what you will. . . . Now you and God love them together.

"Remembering God always is present and always is loving you—for He made you and He made you good and He delights in you—take a few moments to enjoy God's loving you."

I think children find that last part of the prayer easier than most of us adults. When I talked about that with our pastor, his opinion was that they are so fresh from the hand of God that they have only a short way to turn back to be with him. We adults have been coming a long and complicated route through our lives, our society and our complex, technological world. In a sense, we have so many things to consider that we tend to lose the simplicity of the "one thing necessary." Prayer is simple.

Children, too, it seems to me, find it easier to believe in their own goodness. We say we do, but . . . almost always there is the "but. . . ." If we really believe *in* God and believe God, we realize that there is only one God and that is none of us. We are creatures. By definition we are limited, and we are mistake-makers. That does not take away from the fact that God made us and made us good. On the one hand there is no denial of mistakes and sin; on the other hand, there is no denial of goodness. It seems to me that genuine self-acceptance and realization of goodness is a consequence of coming to know God and to love Him. It's a life-long journey.

At the end of the praying session I reminded the parents that they can do this any time and any place—for God is always present and always loving us. What we need to do is recognize and enjoy it. No money, no talent, no equipment is needed. The only requirement is our own receptive heart.

There was no need for them to sit up—all were. I asked them to open their eyes and to spend a moment alone letting what it means wash through them. We concluded with the prayer Jesus taught us to pray.

No one moved. They were very quiet. Softly I asked, "Do you see why your children respond as they do?" They did . . . several with eyes moist.

During subsequent meetings there are always new parents present. So some of this is repeated. Almost always there are new questions, new observations. And almost always there are some parents who are not altogether friendly to the notion. Not initially, they aren't. *"Are you sure this is praying?"* is a question I get asked frequently.

"What is prayer?" is the question I'll ask back. There are so many definitions. Because of the poverty of education in this area, some adults identify saying prayers with prayer. Of course, saying prayers can be prayer. Saying formal, memorized prayers is one good way to pray. It is not the only way, nor does it necessarily—in itself—satisfy all of our prayer needs. We talk about what prayer is: a living, conscious relationship with God; a revealing of ourselves to Him; and a listening for His own self-revelation. Has not Jesus called us "friends" and said that friends know what each other are doing? We talk about prayer as a hunger, a seeking, a journey, a wanting, a longing, a welcoming of God into our very being so that our everyday's living is *qualitatively* affected by our consciousness of His presence. I hope this seeking and questioning never ends, on this side of the grave, for any of us.

One parent who was there for the first time strongly questioned me because of what her children had told her. "Do you hypnotize them?" she asked with some asperity. "It sounds like it to me!" Others present were startled.

"I'll answer you now. I'd like to answer you again after we have prayed together and you have experienced what your children do. For now, let me say this: No, I do not hypnotize them. I would consider that inappropriate, unprofessional, and—under the circumstances—just plain wrong. Is that clear?" The words were; the woman was not convinced. "When we concentrate strongly— whether it is studying, thinking about a problem, being serious in tennis or any sport, or praying—the brain waves are different. Did it ever happen to you, that you were concentrating on something so hard you didn't hear the door bell or the phone or someone calling you? Yes, that had happened to people present. "The brain waves are operating on a different level. We are not so alert nor attentive to all the stimuli around us. We are not as unconscious as we are in sleep, and we are not so controlled as in hypnotism. It is that state to which I invite the children—and you—in prayer. We let go of outside stimuli to a certain degree and attend to our inner selves and the Lord speaking to us in our depths." The parents looked as if that would have to do. It was the best I could manage that day. After the prayer time she seemed a little more at ease about it.

Another parent, at the end of a session, remarked: "I have two children in this school. The seventh grader said he likes the prayer room because it is a time to rest. My second grader said he likes the prayer room because he likes to come here to talk to God in his heart. . . . Both of them are right. I like it for both of their reasons."

Terri responded to her. "Tell them that." Terri smiled. She continued. "Some of you are here for the first time. Let me tell you something. Let your kids know that you came to the prayer room, and that you prayed with God in your heart. It's amazing the things that they tell you once they know you did it too." Several other parents, who had been there before, affirmed her observation. "Mine," one continued, "says God comes to her stomach! But she seems happy about it. I suppose at six a stomach is more important than a heart."

Occasionally parents still express strong feelings about my teaching the children formal prayers to be memorized. One put it this way: "What if they ever end up in a concentration camp? What will they have to fall back on?" I assure them of two things. One is that the classroom teacher teaches formal prayers. They are in the school curriculum which comes from the diocesan office. The teachers do a good job. The second thing is: this is another way to pray and one which might be very good to fall back on. It provides children with options. They can do what is most satisfying for them.

At one evening session there was a couple who reminded me of *American Gothic*. They were solemn, serious, somewhat aloof; I had a feeling they were perturbed. No friendliness emanated from them. During my initial presentation I felt their presence so strongly I was bothered. So I interrupted myself and asked, "Do you want to say something or ask something?"

"Not now," the man answered, "I'll save my questions for later."

After the slides, I asked the parents (as I do the children) to sit back and let one image come back to them . . . just one. After a pause, I ask them to think: why that one? If there are enough couples there, I suggest they tell each other the slide which came and explore it. Sometimes I ask pairs of people to do that. Sometimes I put it into the first part of the quiet prayer . . . to be looked at with God and to ponder the personal meaning in His presence.

On this occasion I had used a good number of the children's images. "You can't help but find God's presence in them" was the remark of the gentleman who had been reserving his questions for later. He paused, then continued with what was troubling him.

From his account I came to understand that at one time he had had an unfortunate experience in a group. His concern and his wife's was about what was happening with the children when I had them sharing in groups. Specifically, were the children being encouraged to blurt out intimate things about themselves and their families? And, if so, children being children, would they use this material later to tease and taunt each other?

What a valid concern! I do so much group work professionally, it never occurred to me to assure parents about that. I had been negligent. I apologized and explained. Working backwards, I began: I never ask the children to talk about anything after we begin with: "Welcome God in your heart." . . . That, I think deserves so much respect that if it is talked about at all, it is done at the child's request, and privately. Even then I advise them to select carefully the person to whom they would confide their prayer. The same is true for you, I told them. It's a good thing to have someone you can trust with these matters, but be as sure as you can it is a person who knows the ways of God and can be of genuine assistance to you in your journey.

As to the rest of the concern: Generally, I just don't let it happen. Whether it be a child or an adult, if people are pressured into saying more than they want to or surprised into blurting out things they would not ordinarily say, they will resent your knowing and possibly go through a period of avoiding or hating you. The truth is, no one has the right to this sort of information without the other person's permission. If a child begins to say intimate, personal, or family things, I stop him/her.

Sister Mary Ann, the principal, was present. She added to the conversation. Mary Ann remembered when she taught religion in the upper grades. During the discussions sometimes children said more than might be desirable. On those occasions, Mary Ann said, she made a strong effort to have the class realize that they were entrusted with something precious. It was not theirs to give away, and so it was to be kept in confidence. As far as she could tell, that had been respected. If any subsequent teasing occurred it was likely she'd know about it and handle it. Mary Ann ventured that the same thing is true in the prayer room.

I think so. If anything from the prayer room were abused, the teachers would be aware of it. They are very aware of the children and what they are doing. Happily the children love the prayer room. Many have said they like it that all the class is praying together, even though it is quiet. At the present time they are not in a teasing stance. (Please God, that will continue!)

The husband of one of the teachers, who works with children in the court system, told me he was quite skeptical when his wife first told him of the prayer room. "Reflection came later in life for me," he said. "I think affirming it in children is dynamite. To let them talk about reflection and to encourage it and make it OK for them is—dynamite!"

His wife, who was present, told me how she uses time after lunch or recess for the children to put their heads in their arms and welcome God into their hearts. Or when they are going to gym or the library, to talk with God in their hearts while they are walking through the halls. "They are precious," Sharon said. "You see their little mouths go, talking to God in their hearts, gesturing, but not making a sound."

One of the mothers described to me how her family prays together every night. It's a solid custom in that house. Their current problem was a relative who had caused considerable pain and trouble to Grandma. The family found it very hard to pray for this relative. How do you wish good to a person like that when what you'd really like to do is. . . ." The sentence went unfinished.

Her child had a suggestion. "Why not put him in our heart and look at him with God and be quiet and see what happens?" The family was trying it, last I heard.

Sometimes the pastor is present, sometimes the principal. They have a standing invitation and always are welcome. During one session John meditated with the parents on Jesus, Mary and their own children. He paraphrased the first chapter of Luke's gospel and had them imagine the infant Jesus and their own child in prayer. We used Psalm 148 for blessing and encouraged parents to bless their children for, under God, they gave them life. Blessings affirm life and ask God to give life fully. At that session we asked the parents present to bless each other. While most of them were a little embarrassed, they did. We ended with 1 John 1–3.

Since we had talked to the parents about blessing their children, I then talked to the children about blessing. They are so accustomed to that being done in church, and by a priest (which is right and good), that the notion of parent's right is a new one.

One of the beautiful things about having the parents come and their being able to talk with their children about what the session meant to them or what struck them is that it provides another entrance into the spiritual development of the child and of the parents, also. When the child genuinely engages in this and when the parent does, both are alive to the life of God in them.

"Don't be afraid of your child's questions," I encourage parents. "And don't expect to answer all of them or to share in all of their experiences. You will have your own. Where you might possibly communicate best is when you come to: "You know what it is like."

This is true of parents and teachers alike. What I fully expect to happen, as this conscious prayer continues, is that the honeymoon phase being experienced will come to an end. Prayer is not always sweetness and light; comfortable and satisfying; it is not always consoling. Arid, dry times come—times when God seems quite absent. That is inevitable. It is a good thing to have a companion during those times. We haven't talked about it yet with either parents or children because they haven't raised it yet. I expect it to come.

In the meantime the PE teacher came to see me. She told me that she always prays with the children before games. Since the prayer room has been in operation, the players ask if they can lead the prayer. Generally, she said, the prayer is well thought out and appropriate. They ask for a good game and that no one will get hurt during it. "At the last game," she said, "the prayer was short: OH GOD, WE WANT TO WIN!"

In Summary

Parents and Teachers Also Need

* to be attentive to their own prayer.
* to have an opportunity to ask questions.
* to be affirmed in their growing toward God.

Prayer

* is, at once, most private and most public.
* has as many valid ways of being as there are praying people.
* allows us to know we are with God, however we are.

God

* has no limits.
* cannot be controlled by us.
* lets us feel His presence at His good pleasure.

Be Aware

God delights in us.
Prayer allows us to enjoy His delight in us.

Chapter 13
What Do I Do?

(On Being Yourself—Using Resources)

Teachers often ask me: "What do I do to reinforce whatever it is I want the children to be using in prayer?"

What each of us needs to do, first of all, is be our authentic selves. It is better yet when we can be ourselves with ease and with pleasure. Each of us needs to say:

"I do some things well; some passably; some poorly; and some I wouldn't even try! I am limited—even in the good things I do."

We cannot give what we do not have. However, I am willing to wager that most of us have much more than we are explicitly conscious of having. Still it is true that what is effective for one teacher is not for another. Let each use what resources are at his or her command. For instance, I cannot sing—even passably well. Therefore, I don't use song with children. Others might use song with fine success. What happens to work well for me is verbal and visual images with music. Several years ago I acquired a camera. It does beautiful things, and I enjoy using it. Now, for me, it is an effective tool for praying with children or with adults.

Once I have decided on the Scripture or topic for a prayer session, I spend some time thinking about how it might be imaged (you might want to find a song which fits). Sometimes images come readily: a series of a potter at work for the potter's story in Jeremiah; or water images with the story of the woman at the well in John's Gospel. Others are more subtle. Sometimes it comes out better than others. Be that as it may, after several years of using these media, I've reached several conclusions:

1. If the images I select make some kind of sense to me, I can count on their making some kind of sense to other people. They

concretize a universal which we experience as human beings. Even though we experience life privately and personally, the experience of gladness or sadness or whatever is a universal experience.

2. The stage needs to be set for the slides (or music) to be received effectively. More often than not I do not speak during the slide presentation. People are prepared to receive the slides by my introductory remarks. What I say is placed in a scriptural context or in terms of the issue we had been discussing.

3. People can be trusted to receive the slides and let the images touch their lives in a unique and personal way. No two people have the same history and experiences; everybody has had human experiences which can be tapped. *Trust them to do it.* Life is a continuing, marvelous reality. Each person's own life responds.

4. Reflection, after the last slide has been viewed, solidifies what might have been received with only superficial attention. Allow time for quiet reflection on the images, especially images which are particularly appealing or distressing. Follow this reflection by consciously connecting it with one's own life, behavior, and experience. Depending on the mix of the group, the intimacy of the topic and the constraints of time (people have to get home for meals, babysitters and the like), I ask them, for their own sake, to say out loud the gist of their reflections. This is not for the other people's information or edification. What research and experience both show is that hearing one's own voice articulate what has been thought about gives it an added dimension of reality. Whether or not feedback is wanted is another choice of the situation and of the moment.

Another (and, happily, inexpensive tool) I use is a slide viewer. It is constructed of cardboard and plastic and uses an ordinary light bulb. On it I display more slides than I can use. For instance, when I knew I was going to use chapter four of John's Gospel, the story of the woman at the well, water was a natural choice. I had photographed a statue grouping of Jesus, the woman, and the well. These I sequenced (Jesus, the woman) according to the reading. Then I added slides of water—symbolizing receiving the living water—for which we are to ask and which comes in any of a variety of ways to us.

Because the research shows that a human figure appearing every seven or eight slides keeps attention on the meaning of the symbol, I am careful to do that. If I have eight slides across a row on the viewer, one in each row will be of a human being. Maybe an extra one will be put in every so often, but at least one human image in a row of eight images is needed.

After the rows are completed, I "read" them. I don't know how else to explain it—I just know pictures can be "read" across as words are, and it is effective in another way.

If I can, I leave the slide viewer set up for a day or two. Maybe three. Perhaps it has to be set on the floor or in a corner at night. Coming back to it several times is not only a pleasure, but new insights come; new arrangements suggest themselves over a period of time. The final product is better for the several viewing times given it.

I "read" the slides several times:

- One reading is for *color.* Too many brights, too many dulls, in a sequence lessens the impact of both. Too many immediate contrasts may be tiring. I move them around to be pleasing and easy in color.
- I read them for *size.* Large, panoramic views of mountains, close-ups where all one sees of a flower is its tonsils, calls for a shift in interpretation of the image. I read them to soften what might be jarring.
- I read them for *shape.* Of course, all are horizontal. (Well, almost all!) Horizontals make for easier viewing.
- I read them for *variety.* Unless that is the intended impact, I won't keep a sequence of exactly the same things. Even with the water slides, I won't use all ocean images, then all rivers, all rain, then all lakes. They will be interspersed.
- I read them for *impact,* for *meaning.* That is the most difficult to explain. All I know is, when I look at them from left to right row after row, I pay attention to my stomach. If my stomach is at ease, the slides are "right." If something sticks and all I think of is "that's pretty," that image doesn't belong, or doesn't belong in that sequence. I don't know how that is, but I know it is a good criterion.

Then insert the slides into a carousel and view it as others will see it. Don't be afraid to do this! After all, we have been exposed to enough media to have some judgment. Trust yourself, and trust the life in your viewers. Remember, the intent is not to go into competition with major networks; it is to facilitate reflection. That is simple.

If you still are not sure, do a dry run. Ask someone else (preferably a person like the people you expect to be present when you use them) to look at the presentation. If it is for classroom use, corral your children or the neighbors' and invite them in for a preview. I don't make it a big event; they may feel constrained to make more criticism than I want to hear! They may even make it up because they think it is expected. Merely present the material, and discuss it as you might with the other real audience. Listening for where it "flowed" and where it "stuck" can be quite helpful.

Timing is essential for the desired effect. I find eight second intervals generally acceptable for most presentations. If it is meant to be very reflective and the group is very quiet, I might go to ten or eleven seconds. Sometimes I pace it to the musical background. On occasion I hold an individual slide longer than the rest of the carousel. If the effect I want is to intensify discomfort, (for instance, if we are dealing with anger in preparation for forgiving) I show slides at five second intervals. It intensifies the unpleasant feelings—especially if the music also is unsettling (eg. "Storm" from *The Grand Canyon Suite;* "Mars" from *The Planets*).

The fun of it is, timing and music can alter the perception of the same slides radically. For instance, for anger I show slides of doors rapidly (at five second intervals) and use Holt's *The Planets,* the "Mars" section. For this context I ask what the door of an angry heart looks like. On another occasion, if I'm using the symbolism of Jesus as a (door)way to the Father—I'll use the same doors with a different introduction and different music (Bach or perhaps Mozart), and show them at ten second intervals. The same images work as well in this very different context.

Music makes a large difference in mood. Ordinarily I use classical or semi-classical music. It is satisfying. It doesn't encourage singing along with nor does it provoke memories as in "our song."

The pace of the music suits the pace of the slides (unless a contrived dissonance is used for effects).

Of course, not everyone will be pleased every time. I am more visually than auditorily inclined. The images appeal to me. At times people tell me the music was so beautiful (that happens more with Beethoven than any other composer I've ever used), that they close their eyes and just enjoy the music!

Whatever visuals you use, use your own judgment. Probably it is more than good enough. Saying you "have no training" is probably not good enough. I don't either. But I do know how to teach, and you probably do too. Apply these skills to another medium.

Let me touch on one last thing. Admittedly, it is a personal judgment. No matter how well the slides are done, how good the recording of great music, these are *not* ends in themselves. Their selection and their use have that in mind. They are not primarily theater or an exhibition. They are ways to facilitate personal reflection and prayer. Sound judgment governs the selection and the presentation. My part is to suggest and to lead. The children, teacher and parents have the option to receive it and let it work for them. My pleasure is in creating the environment, being hospitable and then enjoying with those who enjoy it.

In Summary

What Do I Do about Media?

Do what suites *your* personality and *your* ability!

1. if it makes sense to you, it is likely to make sense to others
2. prepare carefully (media can eat up a ferocious amount of time)
3. trust your own judgment and skills
4. trust others to receive the imagery and symbolism
5. provide reflection time
6. allow time to process and intergrate (rule of thumb: TWICE the presenting time is needed for integration)

If Slides Are Used

1. Set them up on a viewer.
2. "Read" them several times for:
   a. color.
   b. size and shape.
   c. variety.
   d. meaning.
3. If unsure, do a dry run.

Music

Sets, maintains, intensifies, and alters the mood desired.

Timing

Of the slides (five second intervals, or eight, ten or twelve) strongly affects mood and effect.

Be Aware

All media are TOOLS,
not ends in themselves.

Tools are used to achieve a purpose.
- to reinforce a point
- to change the pace
- to be enjoyed
- to help quiet the atmosphere to ready the people present for prayer

It is not necessary to present theater or TV quality shows!

Be yourself! (and, maybe, STRETCH a little!)

Chapter 14

By the Way. . .

(Enjoy!)

"We are all made the same—why should it be different? It all starts when we are children." That statement was made to me by a Cistercian nun to whom I had been speaking to about the children. A number of people had asked me if I found it difficult to go from kindergarten and elementary school children in the morning to adult education in the evening. No, not at all. When it comes to prayer and other things, "We are all made the same—why should it be different? It all starts when we are children."

It is natural to pray. What forms of prayer are best enjoyed is personal. What strikes one as important is partly a function of the person's developmental stage. Teaching kindergarteners through eighth graders makes this very obvious. For instance, at the end of one prayer time, I asked the children to think about what they liked best about God. The youngest said, "He's nice." "He gave me . . . (there followed an assortment of relatives and pets), I like Him . . ., He likes me. . . ." Middle grade children are very aware of fairness. What they liked best about God was: "He's always fair." "He always has time for you." The junior high students said strongly: "You never have to explain anything to Him—He knows." "You don't have to prove anything."

My guess would be that there would be a similarly identifiable progression of values throughout the adult stages, too. I know, in my own prayer, things change as I grow older. For instance, when reflecting and praying from the scripture text on the Beatitudes in Matthew 5, my understanding of them develops. What was important five years ago (according to the scripture journal from then), is still important, but not in a place of priority. What I understand now, I glimmered then. We human beings are on a life-long continuum.

Let's start with the five and six year olds. The younger children have experiences, certainly. We can help them be aware of them and validate their beginning experiences. Their experiences are real. The special languages, words and images can be integrated with their knowing God. Paradoxically, I see this in deep dark and utter brightness. Children, however, are sure of the God experience. The glowing look on the faces of the youngest children when they tell me that "God came to my heart today" is irrefutable. And I find their questions are not questions of the experience but some peripheral thing which is not congruent—for them—with their other experiences.

One time this struck me was when a boy sat up after quiet prayer and said, "That's weird!" What was weird was not that he had known from his grandmother that "it's not time yet," but that his grandmother had bothered to tell him. His grandmother died before he was born—why should she care about him? . . . And yes, he did know what it isn't time for yet. We talked about the reality of the Communion of Saints.

Although our educational system is a good one, at times I find its fault is by way of omissions: omission of strong attention to the spiritual. We educators and parents might feel unsure of ourselves in this or take it for granted. "Of course we believe. Of course. . . ." The "of course" might not be so evident to the children. Certainly it is not found much in TV programs. The good part is that it is so simple to do once we are aware and willing. Some of us need to be persuaded of our own goodness and that what we have in the spiritual realm is good enough.

Acknowledging experience, validating and affirming it, is a basic principle in adult education. It is one I'd urge be applied more to children. Adults are encouraged to attend short term educational events to fill in the gaps of what they know. The assumption is that children don't have enough experience or knowledge to have gaps to fill in. There's truth in that. On the other hand, they have relatively so little experience that what they do have is clear to them: they have less to reflect upon, and so perhaps they can reflect more. Capitalizing on the reality of the situation, listening to their reflections, stretching them to think some more about it and then come back and talk about it is invaluable. Maybe if more of us had been so attended to as children we might have more confidence in ourselves and the validity of our own internal resources.

Besides, when do children of any age come to terms with living with the ambiguity in faith (and the rest of life!) which is vital and realistic? Perhaps it is also a consequence of our scientific age that we explain—unto proof indisputable—and then get stymied when we bump into the mystery of living: ours and God's. A friend who happens to be a clinical psychologist advised me, "Don't explain too much to the children. Do it!" So I didn't, and I did. They responded so well they had no need to discuss who or what God was except in particular context. As when Jane's mother died and her classmates asked, how could this happen and God be good? *Their* context carries it in prayer.

In the adult education technique of brainstorming, any contribution is accepted without comment or need for defense. When considering experience, who can question that the experience was experienced? Why make anyone try to defend the experience? I include children in that statement. At times it might be important to enlarge their understanding of the interpretation of the experience. But as for experience, it stands in its own right.

We all write scenarios to make sense out of what happens to us. For instance, there was the day the fourth graders brought up divorce. That "my real dad only called me once in my whole life" is an experience. *Why* he doesn't call the child is open to interpretation. The child's scenario of rejection might well be enlarged to include other things as it was. Ordinarily, however, when brainstorming, there is no criticism of what is said—by adult or child. In working from it, I still endeavor not to reject an offering if, in any sense, the meaning points in a helpful direction. After all, aren't the Scriptures saturated with meaning, more than scientific accuracies? We have a natural human affinity for meaning. Helping children to attend to their meanings, articulate as far as they can and choose to, is good. We need to help the children to validate their experiences and affirm their continuing reflection. I would like to see this at the heart of prayer education.

One day Frank Wippel, the Diocesan School Superintendent, called and asked if he might interview the children. Both the principal and I were delighted. When Frank came, he stopped a fifth grade boy in the hall and said to him, "Would you please go around the school and collect about a dozen students of different sizes? Sister Mary Ann said it is all right. Ask them to come to the prayer room." Jeff nodded brightly and went off. Within five minutes or so there were a dozen students of various sizes in the prayer room. They also were of different skin colors, different religions, and different shapes. We were pleased.

Much of what came from that interview has already been said. Some of what came from the interview is as yet undone. For instance, the superintendent asked the children if the prayer room makes any difference in the way they attend church on Sunday. So far it seems the children have not made a connection. Nor did I do that with them, explicitly. We have used some Scripture texts (on names, on the name of Jesus, from Jeremiah 18 and the potter, from Job and God's holding the breath of all living things in His hands). These texts I had made into slides and used them several times among the other images. Next year I intend to use more texts and explicitly relate them to the readings of the Sunday liturgy. That is one of the "things-to-be-done."

Another thing-to-be-done is follow-up with the eighth graders. To be practical, it will probably be limited to the youth group in the parish. And a third thing-to-be-done is more work with the parents—for themselves and for family prayer. All of this, however, is simply an extension of nurturing the contemplative in each of us, of living the life Baptism gives us.

Of all the feedback I received, perhaps one comment I most cherish is what some of the children told the diocesan superintendent: "After we leave the prayer room we are nicer to each other."

In Summary

Prayer

- it is natural
- preferred form is personal
- content and values are developmental

Children Experience God

They need validation and affirmation.

Adult Education Principles Fit Children, Relatively

- Their interest prompts the questions for which they are ready.
- Their experiences are indisputable and need reflection and integration.
- Their brainstorming needs to be invited uncritically.
- Consideration may be given to enlarging their interpretation of their experience.

Be Aware

All that any of us have
is our perceptions,
our experiences

with

each other, and
our God

to give love and meaning
to our living.

And that is enough.

Chapter 15

Not Overlooking the Obvious

(Praying)

Once, a long time ago, there was a man named Naaman.* Leprosy was his problem. He went a long way to be cured—a long way, and with many precious gifts for the one who would help him. What happened?

He was told to go and wash in the local river. (People had a habit of washing in rivers in those days, in his country.) Naaman went away angry at instructions so commonplace and simple. His servants were concerned. In effect they said to him: "If you had been commanded to do something difficult and unusual, would you not have done it?" Naaman agreed he would have indeed. "Then why not do the easy thing—go take a bath?"

Naaman got over his huff enough to do the simple thing he was told. He was cured, just as Elisha the prophet said he would be . . . simply.

What has all that to do with us? Well, I wonder how many of us put off really praying until "we are up to it" or "better Christians." I wonder how many of us are putting off praying or praying with others because we aren't good enough or "something or other" enough. Maybe all we have to do, to pray, is to . . . go and take a bath. It's that ordinary.

Look at Jesus. Go through the Gospel accounts noticing when He prayed, where, with whom, and why. Start your list as was done earlier in this book in chapter 9.

---

*See 2 Kings 5:1–19.

Jesus prayed and:

- fed people; provided wine for a wedding party.
- cured people of all sorts of things (including their sins).
- fasted, before He made big decisions (like choosing His apostles).
- asked His friends to stay with Him when He was in trouble (the night before, indeed, He died).
- still wept in frustration because He so loved Jerusalem, and Jerusalem's people would not let Him take care of them.
- forgave all kinds of people, even those who were killing Him.
- wept at His friend Lazarus' tomb, before calling him back to life.
- both thanked and asked his Father for whatever He or the situation required.

Jesus prayed in front of people, with people, for people. He prayed in teaching others how to pray; He prayed in ways we do not know how. What we do know is that He went off alone in the mountains sometimes, and into the desert sometimes; He went off alone to pray. Exactly what happened in those times of solitude? We don't know, exactly. I'm willing to suppose that the times we do know about were as effective as they were because of the times we don't know about—the times Jesus spent alone in prayer.

If we look to Jesus for an example, we can readily see that praying is about as easy as bathing, and as normal. Praying concerns:

- whatever happens (or doesn't) in our lives.
- however we are (or aren't) at the moment.
- whatever we are doing (or not) that day.
- whoever comes to us (or we to them).
- ourselves and our relationships.
- ourselves and our relationship with God.

We are as we are. It is enough for this day. We welcome knowing God's presence, knowing we are with Him:

- saying, feeling, showing ourselves—as we are.
- telling, asking, thanking, praising—as we are.
- waiting, wanting, listening—to receive His Spirit anew.

All of this, too, is about as complicated as Naaman's bathing in the river. Naaman didn't think it was important enough, that river. Perhaps we don't think we, our lives, are important enough to put before God. God does. When we think about it, how dare we let God know that our criteria for prayer, our requirements for encountering our Creator, are more difficult and more stringent than His? That we know better than He does? How arrogant! What an escape from the One who best loves us! What do we fear? Scripture tells us: "God delights in His people." Little children are perfectly capable of explaining that well. After I ask them "Who loves you?" and after they tell me, I ask: "How do you know?" They cite a variety of ways. One is *They like having me around!* What child (of any age) doesn't like being with someone loving? And, at times, to have the loving person all to one's self? (If you had brothers and or sisters, remember the treat it was to have your parents all alone to yourself?)

I suggest it is not so different with God. He likes having us around. Sometimes He wants us all to Himself:

- not only at a large church gathering—though sometimes.
- not only in group prayer—though sometimes.
- not even with an agenda—though sometimes.
- not only with hopes or plans or lists of accomplishments or requests—though sometimes.

He simply wants *ourselves:*

- poor in spirit, but good made better by being close to His goodness.
- poor in spirit, but wealthy in the paradox of having nothing, having all.
- careless, carefree, at the moment creature knowing and loving a knowing and loving Creator.

That is enough—like Jesus going out alone to pray. Of praying, then, I let you listen to something any of us can say to our God:

Planning, pleading
caring, frantic
worrying
complacent
excited
busy, bored, bushed.

In all ways
I come to you.
But—
Best of all—

I come
As do You to me:

alone.

To be together
and have us
to ourselves,

Not even

Planning, pleading,
caring, frantic,
worrying
complacent
excited
busy, bored, bushed
but

together

to ourselves
alone.

Each of us experiences that poignantly, privately with an especially loved person. In this, as in most cases, what is most private
is most usual, for it is deeply human. What I know of loving, you
know of loving; we know it in different ways, with different people,
from different circumstances. What we know of love and fear, anger
and longing we know in our own joy or pain. Yet we all know these

human things. So, too, with knowing God. We can know, if we are willing.

Let's return to Jesus. We know some of how He prayed. We do not know what He did during those times He went out to the desert or mountain, spending time alone with His Father. All the Gospel accounts tell us that He did indeed do that. What might it have been like for Him? I don't know.

What I am sure of is that Jesus and the Father liked to be in each other's company. Sometimes the Father wanted Jesus to Himself.

What I am equally sure of is that the Father likes your company and mine. Sometimes the Father wants you, wants me, to Himself. It is that simple . . . ordinary . . . expectable.

Then, you might ask, "How do I get to do it? . . . how do I get that way?"

The single best answer I know is: Do it! Just, do it!

There are as many ways, I am sure, as there are people. What are you doing when you think you are praying?

- Saying prayers, attending church services? Do it!
- Reading Sacred Scripture? Do it!
- Reading Sacred Scripture, but stopping when something strikes you and explodes in your head and heart, filling you with God's presence, love, fear, tenderness, unity? Do it! Relish and savor it, but do it!
- Reading about other people's responses to God, and thinking how that might fit you? Do it!
- Talking to someone about something, and getting insights into yourself about your situation? Do it!
- Just showing God your heart and being with Him? Do it!

Whatever you do when you think you are praying, do it! Also, leave yourself open to recognizing that perhaps, just perhaps, you are praying more often, and more intently than you might think. Many people do, you know. Prayer, like any communication between people who know and love each other, can be as real and quick as a glance. Especially when it is a glance of a loving heart.

Find your own time and place to be available to your God. Remember it is no more difficult than Naaman's bathing in the river.

One woman I know gets up very early in the morning, puts on the coffee pot, starts a load of wash (she has seven children), takes a cup of coffee to the back porch and sits quietly a while before calling the first son for his paper route and her husband for work.

A man told me has a "ratty old chair," split down the back and therefore covered by a blanket. "God and I meet there an hour a day when I come home from work. Sometimes I read my prayer book. Other times we just talk, or I growl and grumble and yell at Him. Other days we just sit. But you can be sure we meet there— in my ratty old chair—everyday before supper."

Another man said with deep affection and patting his wife's hand, "She got me a kneeler for my birthday. She knows I like to kneel when I adore God." Eileen just smiled and nodded agreement.

There are people who pray while walking or driving or showering, or when doing some ordinary and somewhat mindless household or shop task.

Where does God find you? Often, where you are waiting, He does. But don't count on it. Don't count on controlling the setting (or anything else, when God is concerned)! We can set aside time— lengthy times or glance-length times. A place for prayer may be our choice when we initiate it. Always there is the other side of the coin. When people are lovers, either one can take the initiative. God does, too.

PRAYING

> What does
> God
> bring
> When He
> Comes to me?
>
>> Himself.
>> His Spirit.
>> ("Gifts," some say today.)
>> His Spirit.
>
> What do I
> bring
> When I come
> To my heart's King?

Dare
it be
less
than me?

How like lovers!
Lovers, each bringing
Naked self to
Naked other.

Lovers,
Perhaps not sure
If good enough.

Lovers,
Vulnerable.

And God says:
"Fear not!"
"I delight in my people!"

What does God bring
When He
Comes to me?

And I—what do I bring
When I come
to my heart's King?

Think about it—with God present to you.

God finds us wherever and whenever *He* pleases. Sometimes
His choice of time and place coincide with ours . . . not always.
He comes when He wants. It's up to us to recognize His presence,
and respond as we will.

God is God. Go to the Bible, the Book of Job chapter 42, for
the story of one man's encounter with God. Remember, Job suffered many serious things—the deaths of his wife and children;
loss of extensive property; his health—in miserable, painful ways.
Job's friends were little consolation. Persistently they told him he
must have sinned, so repent! Persistently Job insisted he had not
sinned—there was nothing to repent! They had some strong ex-
changes.

God came. God asked Job where he (Job) was when He created the world. Where was Job when God did a list of God-only things? *Then* Job repented: not because he had sinned the way his friends had accused him of doing, but because he had forgotten God is God. In Job's prayer he says to God how he had heard about Him, but now he *knows* Him for Himself. Job repented for not remembering God is God, and he is creature.

God comes to us, too. When we truly come close we begin to know God—and that is awe-full, for we are creatures. It is awe-full, strengthening, transforming. God yearns for us to come: that is the meaning of His will for us. When close to utter goodness, what is not good about us has to diminish. When close to utter love, what is unloving in us has to change. (Look at the Zacchaeus story in Luke's gospel—Chapter 19:1–10.) Jesus merely came to dinner. His presence, His goodness, was so strong—and Zacchaeus was open and honest enough to be affected by Jesus— that Zacchaeus was moved to give away half of what he owned, and to pay back four times over those he had defrauded. None of us knows what we shall be moved to do when we come close to God. Praying is not flirting. It is a serious relationship with our Creator, one we are meant to have and one which is meant to fulfill us beyond our wildest dreams.

Faith, however, is no light matter. Often enough in praying we might feel nothing and come to wonder: what's the use of praying? Or, perhaps, unfair things are happening to us and living is very difficult. How can God be in this injustice, in this illness, in this misunderstanding, in this unemployment, in this chemically dependent child or spouse? How can He be?

When those things happen to me I turn to Moses in the Book of Exodus, chapter 33 (near the end). Moses asks God to see His face. God tells him no—no one can see His face and live. Moses persists. He insists God can do it if He wants to enough. What does God do? He puts Moses into a cleft of a rock, covers him with His hand, and passes by. God's face is *not* to be seen. His back is.

Over and over I have experienced that in my life. I don't see God's coming to me in the unfairness, illnesses, separations, and disappointments of my life. Later, like Moses, I see His back and then I know He has been there in truth. Faith is not easy. But, it is—oh, so right!

In rereading these pages I can almost sense the dissatisfaction of some readers. After all this, she still isn't telling me how to pray! Well, if telling you how to go pray means putting down words for you to read, then, no, I'm not. There are plenty of good books which do that. What I am putting before you, for you to do—if you are willing—is to pray your own life before your God. What I am suggesting is that, as is true in any sound friendship, you disclose yourself to your God, be still and receive His revealing Himself to you. Let that en-liven your life! Since God created it, no one knows better than He how you might live it to the fullest!

Since you can't give what you don't have, you can't require your children or students to pray this way unless you do. They need a little encouragement. They do need validation and affirmation. "A little child shall lead them," happens daily. Do engage in this praying with the children! They understand. Think about that.

We bring our-selves, as is, and our loved ones, our concerns, our questions, our lives. What happens? All sorts of things.

I know I need to be faithful in being as I am that day in His presence. Often enough that is quite empty. Yet I am accessible to my God. I know I wait, at times more than I like to—and the waiting may be long, tedious and dull, seemingly a waste of time, much of the time. And then:

I know.

I know His presence:
Comforting, glowing, serene, alive!

I know His presence:
Confronting, demanding, insatiable, bone-burning.

I know His presence:
Terrible and terrifying; awe-full, mysterious.

I know His presence:
Creator, Redeemer, Sustainer.

I know
we know and love each other! and each other's loves.

Like all creation, it is very good, indeed.

And so can anyone know—anyone who prays prayer as mutual self disclosure . . . anyone who comes to God in person and who receives God in Person. Again I ask, what do I know?

What do I know?

Color, sight, sound
Feel and taste

As my toes
Squish the warm, brown mud
Under sun-shined water

I splash
and laugh
as I taste and see
How sweet my Lord is

in my
puddles of knowing

I bring
my King

Me.

And, sometimes He
comes and takes me

into His
Cloud of Unknowing

in the Son
we are one.

This I know.

Maybe we don't have to join Naaman in the river Jordan. Perhaps we come to the *Cloud of Unknowing* by splashing around in *Puddles of Knowing.*

In Summary

Praying

- is as ordinary as anthing else in life.
- is relevant to everything in life.
- can be hours long, or glance-time short.

We

- are, as we are; that is enough for this day's prayer.
- do well to find a special place and time for prayer.

How Do We Pray Contemplatively?

- Do it!
- Just, do it!
- Wait, attentively, in case God wants you to understand something now.

Be Aware

God likes us to be with Him.

Sometimes He wants us to Himself alone.

Let us enjoy each other's company—God's and ours!

RESOURCES

Books

Cavalleti, Sofia. *The Religious Potential Of the Child.* translated by Patricia M. Coulter and Julie M. Coulter. New York: Paulist Press, 1983.

Fischer, Kathleen R. *The Inner Rainbow. The Imagination In Christian Life.* New York: Paulist Press, 1983.

Halpin, Marlene. *Imagine That!* Dubuque: Wm. C. Brown Company Publishers, 1981.

Music

For classical (and other) music at excellent prices:
Publishers Central Bureau
Department 273
One Champion Avenue
Avenel, N.J. 07001

For meditative, instrumental, environmental, or/and non-western music:
Music For the New Age
Vital Body Marketing
P.O. Box 703
Fresh Meadows, N.Y. 11365

Adult Programs _____

Shared Faith

Shared Faith is for the single, the married, the divorced, the widowed, and the elderly. It provides the resources and experiential techniques that address adults as adults. Written by Mary Jo Tully, each book in the *Shared Faith* series includes a collection of resource readings for the participants. Following each reading are two or three questions that call for the reader's reflection and how the reading relates to his or her personal life.

Included in each *Shared Faith* book is a guide for the group facilitator. It provides a four-step session outline consisting of an activity focusing on some dimension of the topic, exploring, discussing, and reflecting on the topic; scriptural reading, and prayer. These session outlines include music suggestions and additional discussion starters.

The four books of the *Shared Faith* series are:

Blessed Be

Nine sessions in which adults are urged to discuss the Beatitudes in light of their own experience and belief.

Readings include: Blessed Poverty, Blessed the Gentle, Happy the Mourner, The Hunger Within, Beyond the Law, and Blessed the Pure in Heart. (#1822)

Church: A Faith-Filled People

Ten sessions focusing on the Church as a community where adults share caring, loving, and belonging through God and each other.

Readings include: We Are a Community, Love Does Such Things for Us, With Thanks to the Father, Our Forgiving God, and One in the Spirit. (#1823)

Psalms: Faith Songs for the Faith-Filled

Eight sessions for adults to increase their appreciation of the Psalms and the enrichment they bring to prayer.

Readings include: One with the Father, We Believe, Out of Nothing, Sing a Song of Freedom, and Ever Faithful. (#1824)

No Other God: A Spirituality of the Ten Commandments

Newest in the *Shared Faith* series, this book contains eight resource readings and sessions for reflection upon and study of the Commandments.

Readings include: I Am Lord, My Name Is Holy, A Day in Honor of Yahweh, And the Two Shall Be As One, and Choose Life. (#1942)

Imagine That!

This creative resource discusses imagination, emotions, and phantasies as contributors to awareness, decision making, and motivation. Also covered is the use of phantasies in spiritual direction.

Imagine That! also contains 15 presentations that engage participants in a phantasy and then ask for reflection, meaning, and insight resulting from it. The phantasies can be used by an individual or a group. The phantasies are divided into three sections: Exploring Yourself, Exploring Your Relationship, and Exploring the Terrain Around You. (#1812)

Also available is a 60-minute video cassette which demonstrates and discusses using phantasies. Following that are two phantasies complete with visual reflection/prayer meditation. The video is presented by the program's author, Marlene Halpin, Dominican.

Selected Reading: Religious Education —
Teaching Religion Effectively Program

Teaching Religion Effectively Program (TREP) is a resource to help catechists build confidence in themselves, to develop teaching skills, and to become aware of their catechetical ministry.

TREP provides practical assistance in six areas: communication, development of the learner, lesson structure, educational methods, use of activities, and teaching religion.

The *TREP* Program Manual provides outlines for each of the six two-hour sessions plus optional one-hour sessions that deal with prayer, media, and doctrine. There is also a two-hour Teaching Laboratory. Included are 26 spirit master worksheets and 6 overhead transparencies for use in developing the program.

The *TREP* Essay Book for participants contains readings for the six general sessions and optional sessions. The readings are 10 to 13 pages each and provide background information on the specific concept to be covered.

Teaching Religion Effectively Program is coauthored by Mary K. Cove and Jane E. Regan. Essay Book (#1825) Program Manual (#1826)

Avoiding Burnout: Time Management for DREs

Sound advice on organizing and managing those activities that overwork and overload the parish DRE is the focus of this thorough how-to. It covers such areas as record keeping, communications, workshop planning, accountability, and job description. Included is a 12-month church year/planning calendar with workflow suggestions. Written by Clarice Flagel. (#1782)

The DRE Ministry, Issues and Answers

This handbook for DREs deals with professional questions and ministerial growing pains. Some of the questions this resource answers are: What is a DRE? What does it take? Whom does the DRE serve? What does the DRE do? Some of the issues it responds to are: education, recruitment of volunteers, maintaining relationships, ethics, and accountability. Written by Clarice Flagel. (#1842)

Mending Our Nets

Every program director should have a copy of this complete how-to for the organization and management of a parish high school religious education program. It covers such important considerations as budget, teacher and student recruitment, curriculum, and evaluation. Also included are dozens of checklists, worksheets, and flowcharts. Written by Rosemary Torrence. (#1757)

Theologians and Catechists in Dialogue

The relationship—or lack of it—between Catholic theologians and catechists is the issue confronted in this report of discussions held by twelve knowledgeable representatives from both disciplines. Some of the key areas covered are concerns of each, ways to work cooperatively, and a need for partnership. Edited by Brennan Hill, Ph.D. and Mary Reed Newland. (#1671)

Teacher As Gift

Containing over 40 questionnaires to help assess performance, attitudes, strengths, and weaknesses, this self-evaluation tool also defines and identifies the role of a religious educator. It includes a professional profile worksheet and liturgy for teachers. Coauthored by Sr. Gertrude Ann Sullivan and the San Diego Education Team. (#1729)

Selected Reading: Family _____

Christian Family Almanac

How to make special moments out of holidays, holy days, and even ordinary days is the objective of this resource. It not only tells what days to note throughout the year, but also meaningful ways for the whole family to observe them. Also included are outlines for family rituals and at-home celebrations. Coauthored by Margot Hover and Monica Breidenbach. (#1740)

Selected Reading: Spirituality _____

Year of the Lord, Reflections on the Sunday Readings

Whether for individual reflection or informal group enrichment, these books are for Catholics interested in personal reflection on the three Sunday scripture readings. For each Sunday and major feast of the liturgical year, there is a citation of the readings, summary statements establishing the theme for each, a reflection on a general theme suggested by all the readings, and a prayer response. Written by Rev. Alfred McBride, O.Praem. Cycle A (#1847), Cycle B (#1848), Cycle C (#1849)

Christian Spirituality for the Eighties

This book is a collection of four papers presented at a symposium of religious educators and pastoral ministers. Written by Howard Gray, S. J., Rosemary Haughton, Peggy Ann Way, and Claire E. Lowery, the papers deal with the emergence of pastoral ministry, spiritual growth through pastoral work, the ecumenical and cultural diversities of spirituality, and a pastoral model to renew awareness of the covenant relationship. Edited by Ms. Lowery. (#1940)

In His Light

This readable and concise resource presents the basics of Catholic faith along with current thoughts and trends developing within the Church. Each chapter is preceded by an allegory (which are excellent for meditations) and the book concludes with an index of Catholic prayers and practices. Written by Rev. William A. Anderson. (#1716)

Journeying in His Light

This formation guide presents 35 topics and session outlines. Using chapters from *In His Light* as background, sessions begin with a series of scripture references and include questions for discussion and reflection. Space is provided for composing personal thoughts and prayers. Each session concludes with a simple prayer. Written by Rev. William A. Anderson. (#1858)

For further information about the materials available from Wm. C. Brown Company Publishers please call us or write:
Wm. C. Brown Company Publishers
Religious Education Division
P.O. Box 539
Dubuque, IA 52001
(319) 589-2898